Yorkshire 2035

The New Assembly
A Scenario

With the restoration of our
Dignity
Freedom   &   Liberty

By Steve Mullins

Contents

Dedication

This book is dedicated to those members of my
family who, sadly, are no longer with us.

Acknowledgements

I would like to say a big 'thank you' to all the
people I have met, drunk with, argued with (and
some times listened to) who have rounded out my
thoughts about a Yorkshire of the future – too many
to list, you know who you are and this would not
have been possible without you

In particular, I would like to thank Dr. David
Clegg, an old friend of many years' standing who
understands grammar, can read and doesn't mind
upsetting me. His diligence in ploughing through the
final draft and offering some much needed changes
have improved things considerably.

That said, any inaccuracies, omissions or insults
are mine, and mine alone. You are welcome to bring
them to my attention.

<u>An Invitation.</u>

Whilst writing this short book and reading around the topic – whether recent books, papers or website postings, I have been continually surprised by the number of people since 2020, or thereabouts, who are of a similar opinion – that central government has become so hollowed-out, wasteful and inward-looking that they have lost the plot.

I would like to extend an invitation to all those of a similar opinion in Yorkshire to meet together to consider how, cooperatively, the process of our becoming more responsible for our own actions can be accelerated and rolled out across the County, focusing again on the people and not the already wealthy.

Steve Mullins

January 2024

<u>Foreword.</u>

This book is written for all those who are heartly fed up with the bloated canker-ridden apology that masquerades as a Westminster government; hollowed out with an inability to plan, manage or deliver – other than to a circle of elite cronies.

For Yorkshire this has meant that:

- Instead of a defined strategy, we get multiple policies – amended at a whim.
- Instead of incisive local leaders, we get puppets – dancing to the party tune.
- Instead of meaningful investment, we get promises – and incremental degradation.

For decades, whatever party is in power, cumulatively we have had roughly 80% of the level of investment enjoyed in the south-east.

The poor state of affairs was noted as far back as 1968 by Arthur Wise in his document describing the English civil war where the North rebelled against the South, disillusioned with central government[1].

North fought South with guns and bombs whilst the queen flew over the mayhem with her cronies and hangers-on, oblivious to the inequalities.

Little has changed since then, other than the earlier conflict using guns and bombs has been replaced by money and various media, with the queen replaced by Westminster politicians.

---

[1] The Day The Queen Flew To Scotland For The Grouse Shooting.

The landed gentry and 'posh boys' in London still exhibit a profound lack of understanding about what is happening elsewhere in the country – unless, of course, it interferes with their annual grouse shoot.

Since Arthur Wise, we have had the Barnett formula which bases investment on what was provided the previous year. Consequently under- or over-investment has been exacerbated for over 40 years. The result is that our infrastructure doesn't work, our education suffers and inequality is rife. But, if you're a winner in the south, would you change anything?

The scenario presented here is one where a small group sets out to influence policy decisions with a business-like approach, standing at the 2024 election despite risking lost deposits.

Subsequent elections saw a small cohort of MPs elected to Westminster, where they exerted influence and supported Yorkshire's improvements.

The focus of this story, however, is Yorkshire. The machinations of Westminster have been left for another day.

I hope you enjoy the scenario. Comments, corrections and additions are always welcome, and any errors or inaccuracies are solely my responsibility.

Steve Mullins. January 2024

Introduction.

In 1776, Scottish social philosopher Adam Smith, who is regarded as the founder of modern economics, published *The Wealth of Nations*. In it, Smith promoted an economic system based on free enterprise, the private ownership of means of production, and lack of government interference[2].

It sounded good in 1776 and it sounded better in 2027.

After setting the scene and exploring the turmoil from 2022 to 2027, the story charts three interwoven strands, these being Society, Commerce and the Public Sector; encased in a culture that is Yorkshire and managed through a new social structure for the exclusive benefit of the County.

A County which hitherto had been managed and controlled through a political system some 200 miles distant – a system that had steadily lost its way. By 2022 Westminster had been clearly shown as irrelevant and unfit for purpose but it took a few years to put things right.

The 2024 election had seen a change of party and a change of government focus from reporting and recording to one fighting emergent technology; technology which threatened the very roots of government itself; exacerbated by financial mayhem and government ineptitude.

---

[2] Taken from https://www.history.com/topics/ industrial-revolution/industrial-revolution

By 2024, the time was ripe for a New Order with a new approach to politics – an approach based on:

- Creating a relevant non-party (all party) assembly that represents Yorkshire, not a political ideology,
- The reuniting (reunification) of Yorkshire as a County in three parts (ridings); not as four separate counties, confused by changing boundaries and strange geographic coverage,
- Creating a representative body that is not in any way dependent on Westminster,
- Having clearly written documentation, not the laissez-faire that had been the traditional stuff of English politics,
- Managing a body that brings together disparate Yorkshire people and groups to share expertise and open mutually beneficial opportunities,
- Using emerging technologies, not understood by Westminster, to generate commercial opportunity, positive political influence and regional cohesion,
- Collaborating to generate further commercial opportunity from international events and trends; whether man-made or natural,
- Establishing financial probity and investment in projects that matter to Yorkshire society, properly controlled in a professional manner,
- Moving the balance of the many making the few richer to a more equitable division of wealth, also mindful of an ageing population.

This is the story of how that transition of power took place between the years 2024 and 2035, starting with the 2024 election.

In the run-up to the 2024 election, increasing numbers of pockets of discontent had formed – spurred on by the mendacity of Westminster and social inequalities. A number of new parties formed in readiness for the election.

The 2024 election saw the Tories removed from power and Labour elected – but with a smaller majority than forecast and dependent on the Liberals and Greens to get bills through Parliament.

With self-interest at the top of the list, the Liberals and Greens now demanded a form of Proportional Representation (PR) to get their numbers in parliament up to the level they merited from votes cast. This would give them a much stronger representation at the next election.

Technology, in particular social media and artificial intelligence (AI) were being manipulated to an unprecedented level causing significant problems for those in power. Such was the pressure from technology (and with PR in place) that an early election was called for in 2027.

The 2027 election, with the benefit of PR, saw a number of new Yorkshire MPs elected and a more representative government where the balance of power could now be more readily manipulated.

These Yorkshire MPs subsequently banded together to anticipate Westminster's manoeuvrings and worked to advise the New Order.

The New Order took the form of an assembly working alongside conventional politics and interlinked with society and commerce.

The Assembly's objective was to reunite Yorkshire administration and society under a written constitution with investment directed to enriching the County though the encouragement of, and support for, entrepreneurship – taking advantage of alternative financial instruments to support new and emerging opportunities.

This is the story of how it happened.

Part 1 –Governance Reconsidered.

Changes throughout the world, as well as within Britain had taken the traditional style of government (opposing, adversarial parties) beyond breaking point.

A dependency on external consultancies and the global ineptitude of senior politicians has become increasingly evident and a new form of government needed to be considered.

Driving Forces.

External (World) Forces.

Dissent, territory and a desire for power during the years leading up to the 2024 election led to various international conflicts; all of which had a destabilising effect and a disruption to normal life in the UK.

Disruptions, whether through refugees, energy shortage or international financial commitments, all gave the government of the day issues to contend with in addition to running the country.

Technology in all forms whether electronic, medical, chemical or defence affected all aspects of government and social life. The various impacts of technology on different aspects of life were many and varied, but all inescapable.

The government's inability to regulate or control technology became an important consideration. Elsewhere the 80-year cycle[3] is discussed and the transition from reporting to invention. Governments through the decades have been too slow to regulate emerging technologies and too isolated to control technologies developed abroad.

The Covid pandemic changed the nature of UK society in many ways, be it health, education, socialising, commercially – the list goes on.
It also exposed significant weaknesses in the government of the day and in government in general, some of which is discussed below.

Climate change had been in evidence for over forty years but for a significant period of time the impact had been ignored, denied or used to deflect weak governance, the degree of change has been the subject of debate[4] and many learned papers.
Whatever the pace of climate change, it demanded attention by governments through various agreements but was impossible to regulate (especially) because it is global; however, it offers opportunities for new commercial developments.

The deregulation of the banks by Thatcher & Reagan opened the way for major investments – using fiat money[5] and a risk of overtopping the

---

[3] *Yorkshire 2027* Pg.10 ff.
[4] e.g. Judith A. Curry. *Climate Uncertainty and Risk.*

Fractional Reserve[5] which became evident 30 years or so ago in 2008 and damaged the UK (and world) economy for more than 20 years, leading to 'difficult decisions[6]' such as *austerity* which are noted below.

Not long after the 2008 meltdown, the invention of blockchain currencies came about with Bitcoin as, perhaps, the best known.

2024 was a significant year for blockchain (crypto) currencies in that their inventors had claimed that, because they were distributed, no-one was responsible for scams and fraud (unlike the banks). This was challenged in the courts and, because any changes/decisions were controlled by just half a dozen or so people, the ruling was that these currencies were centrally controlled and subject to making good any customer losses. This created international turmoil around, and beyond, the time of the 2024 election[7].

Many natural resources are quite rare, or their supply closely controlled, leading to imbalances in international negotiations – negotiations where the UK government had demonstrated staggering ineptitude and much wasted time, energy and money.

---

[5] For a discussion on fiat money and Fractional Reserve banking please see Appendix 1, part 3.

[6] Difficult for those with little, not so difficult for the well-heeled in Westminster and their cronies.

[7] Please see also Appendix 1, part 2.

To offset some of the potential supply issues, Circular economics was something discussed in lofty terms but with little understanding.

Energy supplies became less secure with the various wars involving some of the world's richest reserves. Despite commitments to cut back on CO_2 the UK had a significant dependency on gas and oil due to a historic lack of investment in alternative sources (hydro, tidal, nuclear, solar etc.) over the last 40 years; this had left the government scrambling for supply and paying over the odds for it.

Ministers were expected to operate under all the constraints noted above (with very little training in managing any of the disciplines), plus a top-heavy administration. All exacerbated by the winning party having to administer the internal affairs of the UK as well as compete (pointlessly) with the other political parties in the UK.

Internal (UK) Forces.

The lead-up to the 2024 election highlighted the government's lack of capability and their making it up as they went along, too readily shuffling off responsibility, creating unnecessary work and fostering delay – all at a cost to the public purse.

The one feature which probably emphasised the aloofness and lack of contact was growing inequality where those with the least were charged with paying proportionally much more for the poor decisions and profligacy made by those with the most.

["I share your pain" – A comment from wealthy New Yorker, Alexander Boris de Pfeffel Johnson, uttered on more than one occasion].

It was inequality in all its forms (levelling-up, Northern Powerhouse etc.) that led to 'difficult decisions' by Westminster – but difficult for others, and brought about serious dissatisfaction and a loss of faith by many in the government of the day.

The need to hide[8] increasingly poor decisions grew and grew up to 2024 as the various cabinets became increasingly bungling which had made some earlier Prime Ministers and politicians actually look quite competent (not easy).

Yorkshire 2027 enumerates many examples of the catastrophic cock-ups, failures & promises wrought upon the UK by a detached, privileged & out of touch series of Prime Ministers and their dim witted[9] cabinets. Below is an abbreviated list:

<u>Some of the bigger ones.</u>
- Track & Trace – cost c.£30bn,
- Protective Clothing (Covid) £15bn written off (FT Jan 26 2023),
- Liz Truss' budget – cost c.£30bn,
- HS2 overrun - £40bn (at least),

---

[8] The blame culture and media scrutiny meant that politicians are supposed to be infallible, such that only minor decisions are made with an inept cabinet.

[9] Bigger decisions being made by consultancies (Alan Johnson. *In The Thick Of It*. ISBN 978-0-00-842226-4

- HS2 cancellation - £30bn,
- The NHS (enough said),
- Brexit – c.4% of GDP per annum cumulative,

<u>Some of the (relatively) smaller ones.</u>
- Horizon (Post Office) 3 different compensation schemes - £43m plus legal costs; innocent people imprisoned,
- Nightingale Hospitals – c £500m,
- Supply chain awards - £10m to a mate with no experience and no boats,
- 3,000 jobs lost at Tata Steel in South Wales.

This list could go on with payments of tens of millions to cronies and supporters.

<u>Some where data is dubious or irrelevant.</u>
- Horizon compensation, contaminated blood, WASPI Women – none resolved,
- HS2 blighting the lives of many who can't sell their homes and move on,
- The mis-management of Covid,
- Damage to education, NHS, society etc. etc. – not listening to advisors,
- Covid parties in Downing Street (£50 fines for MPs; £,000s for citizens),
- Honours lists, featuring foreigners who sue our government and others 'moved out of the way'.

<u>Some of the more local ones.</u>
- The A64 – no action over 40 years despite repeated promises,

- Fracking & Solar Farms – locally very damaging, but supported by local party MP who has to be seen to be loyal,
- Villages isolated – lack of investment in public transport,
- East-west rail journeys – a joke,
- Moves to build on Areas of Outstanding Natural Beauty (Moors, Dales, Wolds) – not very relevant in London,

It is against this backdrop that government had tried to operate, hide mistakes, pretend to know what they were doing and all the time confounded by events. As they attempted to manage and control all the above forces, and look as if they were in charge, credibility crumbled[10] along with internal discipline, support for society, and investment in commerce – other than services, consultancy and banking.

Lack Of Control, Loss of Credibility.

Leading up to the seminal 2024 election the impact of both external and internal forces on the ability of government to manage was immense.

Their ineptitude is discussed in an earlier book (Yorkshire 2027); sufficient for this discussion is to recognise that an aloof elite, detached from normal society and from commerce who lack experience and understanding have little or no chance of managing this level of complexity.

---

[10] See *Yorkshire 2027* Pg.22 Peter's Principle Revisited

This ineptitude had been exacerbated since the mid-1990s by an increasing call on the 'big six' management consultancies which had incrementally 'hollowed out' collective knowledge and experience in government (and also commerce) – in the process increasing dependency upon consultancy whilst also opening the door to additional (normally lucrative) follow-on business[11].

A new type of politics was needed; one where each played to the others' skills. A trust built between not only government, society and commerce but also with other political parties, calling on each others' experience and skills.

It had been shown time and again that adversarial politics had stopped working (just watch Prime Minister's Questions on a Wednesday).

Selfishness beats altruism within groups, altruistic groups beat selfish groups. Everything else is commentary.

Evolutionary Biologists, Wilson & Wilson.

---

[11] Often with conflicting interests. See *The Big Con* pg. 149ff. Infantilising Organisations

The Need For A New Order.

For government, things are not going to get better, or any easier. We saw the migration of yet more wealth to the select few force increasing borrowing, associated high interest rates for the many and more crime driven by necessity.

Technology provides additional opportunities to increase profits (and scams), consultancy removed collective knowledge and understanding from government, new external threats and the very nature of ponderous centralised policy-making made new regulation all but impossible.

Add to that how government, like so many large and long-established organisations, (appeared to) lose sight of their underlying purpose; which, if not lost, is unclear or they have failed to communicate it.

One solution was a degree of decentralisation and local cooperation which is discussed later.

First some of the factors that acted to destabilise established economies, including that of the UK.

<u>Rapidly Evolving Events. A Selection.</u>

In considering outside influences it is normal to have the 'good actors' and the 'bad actors' where a new development, or technology, provides not only the beneficial results it was designed for, but also opens opportunities for abuse by those wanting to disrupt society or seeking personal gain at the expense of others.

An obvious example is nuclear energy which can safely produce usable power (good actor) but also be harnessed to deliver devastation (bad actor).

Increasingly, the role of government was to promote the good actor (investment) and hinder the development of the bad actor (over-regulation). These activities demanded experience beyond that of the career politician. A few are noted here.

<u>Artificial Intelligence (AI).</u>

AI is an enormous field with vast sums spent on its development by multinational companies such as Google and Microsoft with new applications which were many and varied, from writing exam papers for inadequate students through to safely driving cars. Artificial intelligence cropped up in just about every setting to influence decisions and ways of working[12].

An additional impact of technology (along with excessive consultancy) was the taking over of jobs and the associated redundancies in government, and multinationals – which also served to increase their reliance on consultancy and technology.

<u>Finance And Currencies.</u>

Governments of all persuasions had abused the financial system, encouraged to do so by donors, big business and the banks.

---

[12] See bibliography for a selection of publications.

Added value went to the privileged few (as shareholder returns) when that money ought to have been providing benefit to the people[13].

Around the year 2024 crypto currencies and on-line banking were losing favour (people defrauded by crypto, inflation) and the fraud (and Ponzi schemes) that is world banking about to collapse[14].

Despite denials, politicians and bankers had been deeply involved in Crypto, using it to back up dodgy mortgages (again). As repossessions grew, property prices fell, global financial markets – mainly mortgage driven – also fell, banks failed (again) and governments had to bail out indebted home owners.

Local hard currencies (e.g. the Lewes pound), time banks and local crypto were beginning to gain some traction to the point that government was losing control of its own treasury (more of this later).

Medicine (and Pharma).

A number of developments came to fruition in 2024 which included gene splicing, synthetic biology, cloning, personalised medication and organ regeneration. Surgery could be performed at a distance and specialists deployed from home.

These developments had immense power for good; or, in the wrong hands, could cause immeasurable damage as they became increasingly available.

---

[13] Please see page 399 ff. of *Beyond Money*
[14] Please see Part 7.3.

Responsible organisations ran to similar rules to those adopted by Bill Hewlett and David Packard who established a major IT organisation, starting from their garage[15].

<u>Agriculture.</u>

One application to offset climate change had been the development of ploughing techniques with variable depths to the furrows and the direction and angle at which the field was ploughed at different times of year allowed water retention during the drier seasons and enhanced run-off during the abnormally wet ones.

Other examples included genetic manipulation to create new strains quickly – strains that were drought tolerant, higher yielding, insect resistant or exhibiting other characteristics which benefited humanity.

Some of the big agricultural companies were looking to the welfare of people whilst others were seeking to maximise income by developing a sterile F1 (first generation) so new seeds had to be bought each year.

There was a need for international regulation to ensure that in the rush for profit harmful strains were properly removed.

---

[15] See Appendix 2 ' The Rules of the Garage'.

<u>Energy And Raw Materials.</u>

As barriers to trade increased and natural resources become scarcer the need for innovation grew, whether that was making things smaller, less energy demanding, providing opportunities for alternative (renewable) energy sources, circular economics or carbon capture and storage.

Government needed to direct resources wisely, not only to support the population but also to offer opportunities to SMEs and entrepreneurs for commercial exploitation and to generate income ahead of expenditure.

The means to invest in SMEs and local entrepreneurs was found by overcoming the bankers' caution. One approach had been to increase the use of the Post Office which had kept branches open during the retail banks' High Street closures, a more radical alternative was to open a new bank (see below).

<u>Consultancy.</u>

Since the mid-1990s The 'Big Four' (or 'Big Six') consultancies had insinuated themselves firmly into government and also major commerce.

Their impact had been to reduce or remove decision-making capability and also change focus such that by 2005 energy was redirected from creating benefits and customer satisfaction to maximising shareholder value.

Because the same consultancies were making significant earnings advising both government and industry (sometimes as a conflict of interest) people had been forgotten, industry hollowed out and government infantilised.

Meanwhile, the consultancies found ever increasingly lucrative projects while government lost not only capable people but also its accumulated experience, knowledge and understanding[16].

Governance resorted to propping up bankers (closely allied to elected politicians) through weak regulation, investing in service companies (consultancies) and allowing infrastructure to crumble in the drive to maximise 'stakeholder value' – whatever that was!

---

[16] *The Big Con* Pg 149ff.

<u>Interim Summary.</u>

All the above scenarios, and many more, needed increasing levels of control, audit and management which demanded a wider range of skills, experience and knowledge than that of any one organisation or discipline. The complexity (and interconnectedness) that mushroomed around 2024 and a little way beyond involved and included:

- Technology,
- Finance and currencies,
- Medicine (and Pharma.),
- Agriculture,
- Energy & Raw materials,
- Trying to take back decision-making,

The rise in complexity and fall in understanding had led to some 20 years of 'pretend activity' – creating a lot of heat and not much light (by tinkering around the edges), writing plan after plan after plan (none with any real purpose or direction) and commissioning a plethora of studies, reports and surveys (most of which had delivery dates after the next election), none of which were implemented.

All of which had kept Westminster busy, allowed cronies to maintain the status quo (shareholder value) and starved the country of meaningful decisions and investment.

This had to change.

<u>Some Further Considerations.</u>

There was then, and is now, poor (if any) communication by the major political parties of their fundamental purpose i.e. their core objective – just a reliance on people continuing to vote for them. This was on the point of being challenged.

The result had been that leadership, based on a series of policies which can change depending on public opinion (or press coverage), had led to a time of uncertainty by commercial investors and a loss of trust by the electorate.

Control had been over-centralised to the point that the regions were micro-managed with Westminster having to approve the most mundane of local decisions; Westminster could also overrule local decisions – decisions that had been made for the benefit of a local community.

It is recognised that national interest plays a part in policy-making but examination of options, closer to home had rarely been considered unless an MP or grandee had felt personally threatened by a decision-in-the-making.

The core considerations that now needed to be addressed included:
- Clarifying long-term purpose and intent,
- Building trust,
- Cooperating with other parties, commerce and academia,
- Promoting capable leadership and internal control,
- Learning, not blaming,

- Adopting a culture of transparency,
- Tightly controlling the various media (more of this below),
- Developing greater agility,
- Planning with greater resilience,
- Ensuring adequate regulation.

Part 2. Defining The New Order.

The old-fashioned way of doing politics saw its demise in 2024; so much was out of step with events with an inept management drawn from the elite – once called 'the great and the good' – controlling events with us ordinary mortals seen as insignificant, other than as tools for making their friends rich.

For example, very few of our ministers for education have had any experience of state education outside the serried walls of Eton or, occasionally, Harrow; yet they have defined over the decades how education for the masses should be managed!

Interestingly, when you ask 'what is the purpose of education' no-one seems able to provide a meaningful answer other than 'to prepare youngsters to pass exams'. Cynically, Eton might be considered the exception in that its purpose clearly seems to be in preparing children for government[17].

Ruling Cabinet Inadequacy.

Alan Duncan[18] a long-standing MP came away from the Conservative Party when he experienced the calibre of Prime Minister and the (in)abilities of advisors (Cabinet) whose inadequacies he described in remarkably candid and derisory terms.

The theme seems to have been that Prime Ministers appoint people less able than themselves such that they (PMs) can always look superior.

---

[17] Please see also the footnote at page 102

[18] *In The Thick Of It*

A New Order needed to have leaders who could take advice, act decisively and if a mistake is made, acknowledge that mistake, learn, correct matters at the first opportunity and move on.

In short, a culture of learning was needed to replace the established culture of blaming.

Policy On The Hoof.

The driving focus and direction for decades was policy which, within a few short years changed from record investment in infrastructure, transforming education, encouraging saving (pension funds) and investing in innovation into halving inflation (that they created), growing the economy (having left Europe), reduce government debt (from servicing cronies), cut NHS waiting lists (due to underinvestment) and stopping the small boats[19].

How on earth could someone intending to invest in manufacturing in this country have the confidence of long-term certainty and support? They couldn't.

Policy had been increasingly influenced by the media, crafted to retain 'popularity', abused for personal reasons and (unsurprisingly) failed to deliver any communicable long-term objectivity.

Objectives that should have been enduring, providing longer term certainty and didn't provide much 'wriggle room' or opportunities for excuses.

Policies, pledges and initiatives sound good but were be changed on a whim.

---

[19] The Prime Minister of the day had family in Southampton; draw your own conclusions.

The Dream Of Independence.

In the increasing complexity of modern life, control needs to be carefully crafted; yes, we do need central control for some things but much could be put out to the regions.

The New Order was considered as a forum – a stepping-stone to independence – in that it's goal was to bring a range of people and organisations under the one roof with the aim of exerting sufficient influence to bear in Westminster and locally to ensure that Yorkshire got the support it deserved.

In return, Yorkshire got that support, delivered appropriately, transparently and according to a long-term plan – the start of a move away from an over-centralised government and transitory policies.

In providing support appropriately the needs, opportunities and aspirations of the many needed to be taken into account and dwarf those of the elite; this is rarely seen as the domain of the career politician; many of whom are still considered narcissistic, parochial and occasionally corrupt.

A New Breed Of Representative.

A core 'board of management' was established, drawn from society, commerce and academia – team players selected for ability, experience and competence who were respected, listened to, believed and acted on.

Not the career politicians who had been in no other job and had little experience outside local and central administrations.

Meanwhile, Social Media and 'on-line' living had become a significant feature during the 2000s but by the mid-2020s it became an organ of *fake news* misleading information and political influence – some people discovered that if they had enough followers the social media platform paid them for advertising space; some of these people, in order to increase followers and revenue, posted lies, sensationalism and salacious propaganda in order to drive numbers for personal gain.

These sensationalisms and fantasies needed to be identified, called out and neutralised.

The New Order developed a means to retain honesty by verifying what was posted across a range of platforms even though they could not control them; also a means was created for people to be able to verify anything the Order itself posted.

This demanded the establishment of a team of people working cooperatively, across parties and who, between them, included commercial understanding, technical background, academic integrity and communication experience.

Evolving, Changing & Adapting.

The new Forum, learning from the failure of policy-driven government, managed by combative MPs whose constituencies got left behind in toeing the party line, devised a more business-like approach to governance.

In creating the agile[20] Forum a number of different strands were developed.

These included:

- Developing and communicating a clear and simple objective[21],
- Preparing a written constitution to give clarity to the various roles and responsibilities,
- Assembling a management team from society, commerce and academia focused on Yorkshire, not their own personal benefit,
- Delivering support according to need,
- Providing non-financial support,
- Giving encouragement to innovation in value adding sectors including manufacture,
- Developing marketing opportunities UK & overseas,
- Promoting alternative sources of finance & investment,
- Broadcasting a compelling message to attract followers, and
- Establishing the means to better regulate the media in all their forms.

---

[20] *"The Big Con[sultancy involvement] is preventing governments and businesses from evolving the capabilities they need to transform our economies for the common good ... we need the organizations that make up our economies to ... take bold steps to mitigate the breakdown of our ways of life.* The Big Con Pg. 235

[21] By definition, you can only have one objective; given several, when one falters attention switches to another and little gets completed.

Part 3. Establishing The New Order.

The start point is a clear objective which provides purpose and a reason for people to become engaged with the emerging forum. Here, the objective was developed from the commercial approach which follows the journey:

Vision
Mission
Objective
Strategy
Tactics.

The Vision was developed from a need to deliver principally intangible (life-style?) benefits which were considered under three headings:

- Confidence – that work (and funds) will be there and there is a future to look forward to.
- Reassurance – that daily life continues without worrying about what's round the corner.
- Peace of mind – that services will be fit for purpose, properly maintained and available to all according to their need.

However, these benefits demanded tangible support in the way of finance, assets and resources.

Vision Statement.

Our Vision is *that Yorkshire society has a stable present and a secure future where there is growth and prosperity appropriately supported by our various public bodies.*

<u>Mission Statement.</u>

Our Mission is *to put in place the means to capture the emerging needs of our various societies, recognising and making use of their existing assets and capabilities.*

To influence those in appropriate positions to make available the additional physical and financial resources to ensure that each society's emerging needs can be satisfied in an efficient and timely manner.

To continue to build support for a Yorkshire Forum.

<u>Objective.</u>

The objective delivers defined benefits and is SMART. i.e. **S**pecific, **M**easurable, **A**greed, **R**ealisable (there is sufficient market to make the outcome worthwhile) and, finally **T**ime-bounded.

Our objective is *to have in place, established in the Yorkshire communities and in centres of political influence, the people and technology to collect and process the data that defines current circumstance in order to bring appropriate influence to bear that will rectify immediate issues and open the way for future personal, community and commercial development.*

Not working alone but with other parties, commerce, academia and society.

The strategy is discussed in detail later.

Given the objective and reason for being, the purpose & expectations were clearly communicated to those wishing to become engaged.

<u>Need For A Written Constitution.</u>

In the formative years, the movement was not a political party but a disgruntled and concerned group who could see that things could be made more equal and supportive for Yorkshire.

The career politicians were not yet interested[22], as had been attested by how few attended, or even gave attention to, emerging movements and concerned groups; even the MPs collective *One Yorkshire* was impotent due to the need to toe the line on party dogma.

Those involved came from various backgrounds involving industry and not-for-profit; these various backgrounds supported a constitution directed to efficiency and delivery (see also below *The Precautionary Principle*).

The core element of the constitution paralleled the commercial board of directors with an additional post that mirrored the Chief Executive Officer (CEO)[23] The Officers comprised:

- Leader (Managing Director),
- Chair (Chairperson),
- Nominating Officer (Company Secretary),
- Treasurer (Finance Director),
- Planning Officer (CEO),

---

[22] There was nothing for them personally in the immediate future.

[23] For a more complete discussion about the constitution of a Board of Directors please see *Beyond Money* Pg.247 ff.

Simplistically, the Chair and Nominating Officer ensure compliance and ethical management (the past), the Leader drives the organisation (the present) and the Planning Officer opens future opportunities in line with the agreed strategy (the future).

The Planning Officer would become increasingly important during the national shift to invention and development.

The constitution had formalised the vision, mission and objective; considered the moral and ethical framework, defined membership criteria, established the various Officers and laid out the internal administration[24].

The Management Team.

Working with the Officers was a management team drawn from a variety of occupations and organisations. This group did not come together from day one but grew from a few interested individuals.

Initially, a small number of people who had been involved in discussions and seminars concerning Yorkshire and with a desire for a more equitable treatment than that they were getting from elected politicians who were supposed to represent their needs and aspirations.

Subsequent conversations and memberships drew interest from members of Yorkshire-centred societies and individuals with a desire to do something to support the County.

---

[24] A more complete version is provided at Appendix 3

<u>Building A Presence.</u>

This initial small cohort identified a few people prepared to actively progress the Forum – to go beyond attending the odd meeting and voicing an opinion to putting in time to develop the Forum and sufficient in number to establish a management core which comprised:

- The Secretary (Organising & Recording),
- Rotating Leader,
- Provisional Chair.

Initially, a few people attended hoping for gain, companies looking for customers, politicians hoping for influence, egotists looking for exposure. They soon left and subsequently, not-for-profit groups became involved because they could see benefits and useful contacts for their members. These groups included:

- Specific interest – North York Moors, heritage,
- General interest - Yorkshire Society, 2 Ridings,
- Charitable interest – Rotary, Buffaloes.

Amongst the early adopters were a number of commercial groups, some introduced by the self-interested people who arrived early on the scene. These included:

- Industrial bodies – Chambers of Commerce,
- Economic clusters – Purchasing consortia,
- Commercial firms – SMEs, Established traders.

By 2026, the Forum had grown to a sufficient size and level of influence to begin to offer memberships; the income from memberships allowed additional posts to be created which were filled sequentially as funding permitted. These were:

- Communications Executive (Marketing),
- Media Specialist,
- Intelligence (Analysis & Implications),
- Personnel & Compliance.

Volunteers, donors and supporters were all actively encouraged to join and actively participate, a second programme was established through the website to keep those on the periphery informed and opportunities regularly provided to encourage active participation (however modest – e.g. leafletting).

This 'invading army' was described as a bunch of enthusiastic, disaffected, grey warriors – but they got a lot done; they reached further into communities, provided expertise, supported administration and, in some cases, donated generously.

<u>Establishing The Forum.</u>

Having established a presence and a degree of gravitas, along with media specialisation (including a website) the Forum could reach out to many more potentially interested parties. The tools used were:
- Reports,
- Website,
- Traditional media,
- Social media (verified),
- Published articles,
- Think Tanks,
- Thought Pieces,
- Podcasts,
- In-house experts.

Which were developed here and used later with good effect to influence Westminster and others.

<u>Delivering support according to need.</u>

The exponential growth of Artificial Intelligence (AI) had made it more readily available; having a Forum that represents the County, and with people skilled in IT, it had been possible to dispassionately analyse the varying needs forwarded by different regions and associations.

The debate had always been to assess whether infrastructure is more important than education or whether education is more important than health care for example.

The use of AI alongside discussion and debate helped to clarity where best to invest and also to overcome various individuals' skills of persuasion.

<u>Non-financial support.</u>

One of the handicaps to establishing, or growing, an organisation whether business or otherwise has been uncertainty over what are, in reality, quite minor matters[25]. Because of this uncertainty organisations might not grow as effectively as they should but an informal conversation with an expert e.g. an accountant or a lawyer can readily overcome these hurdles.

By bringing different groups together informally, supported by experts, presentations and seminars, members enjoyed a faster rate of growth than would otherwise have been the case.

---

[25] For example, 'do I do the accounts myself or employ a bookkeeper?'; 'how long before I have to pay VAT?'

<u>Encouragement for innovation.</u>

Innovation can take a number of forms, whether a new product, an extension to a product or a modification of a product in order to enter a new market.

The act of sharing ideas, concerns and difficulties opened solutions to the various challenges and provided opportunities for innovation – supported by people who had appropriate experience to guide, support and encourage.

<u>Developing marketing opportunities UK & overseas.</u>

With two deep water ports, Middlesborough and Hull there were established links into Europe and European organisations. The Forum provided a place for people to discuss needs and share opportunities for export.

It was acknowledged that, for marketing purposes, export was considered to be anywhere outside Yorkshire in addition to overseas territories.

This is relevant in the way the marketing was conducted and also for the development of a financial instrument outside Sterling.

<u>Alternative sources of finance & investment.</u>

Money and banking are discussed later in some detail because it's what makes things happen or allows things to happen.

At the juncture of establishing the Forum there was active study into understanding various forms of transaction from time-banks through local currency to a crypto currency and a 'Bank of Dave'.

None is new all can, and were, applied to create a more influential and equitable Yorkshire.

A Compelling Message.

The message was short and simple, worded to bring out the three core emotional needs noted above which are Reassurance, Confidence and Peace of Mind.

Join us in our mission to work with others to influence Yorkshire politics for a fairer deal, reassured that you will get what's right, have the peace of mind that you will be treated fairly and the confidence to plan for your and your family's future.

Media Management & Control.

By 2024 technological development had reached a level of sophistication that could readily baffle and confuse if not used wisely.

Earlier experiences included American elections, changing the speed of video clips and posting misleading information including *Truth Social*.

Media, in all formats, had been earning money by posting silly, scurrilous, sensational or downright wrong material – the dafter the better as the broadcasters' payment was determined by the number of viewers and followers who read the adverts included in the copy.

Many people's attachment to social media was such that they accepted what was posted without going to the trouble of verifying the content[26].

The situation led to two strands of activity within the Forum, one was to use social media extensively posting appropriate (accurate) material to gain followers and members, the second to reference all material posted by the Forum on a secure website where people could check that the social media content was real and not fabricated for reasons of sensationalism or profit.

AI and overcoming the manipulative use of social media are activities used by many, understood by few and designed to mislead a fair proportion.

A high level of technical capability was required in order to be credible and consistent; the individual who took on the role was assured of a future within the Forum.

---

[26] Please see *You Are What You Read* Jodie Jackson.

Finding A Name.

An appropriate old term for this type of Forum was researched and chosen to reflect the heritage of the County.

The name selected was **The Thing**, also known as a **Folkmoot**, **Assembly**, and **Tribal council**, was a governing assembly in early Germanic society, made up of the free people of the community presided over by a lawspeaker. [Note *Free* People].

The term *Thing* is still found in Tingley – the mound where the council was held near Morley and just south of Rotherham is Laughton en le Morthen and Brampton en le Morthen – *Mor-thing* 'assembly of (the people) of the moors[27]

The name also finds its way into the Isle of Man's Tynwald – (the field of the Thing[28]). The oldest parliament in the world at over 1,000 years old.

---

[27] *Yorkshire place names* pg. 52
[28] https://en.wikipedia.org/wiki/Tynwald

Establishment And Recruitment.

From the outset there were three major concerns:

- Finding the finance,
- Promoting the cause and
- Finding recruits.

<u>Finding the Finance.</u>

With the vision, mission and objective clearly articulated people knew what to expect and could readily decide their level of interest.

The benefit was that those getting involved had a greater degree of commitment, purpose and involvement than someone just thinking 'this sounds like a good idea', they were more likely to be prepared to contribute not just financially but also with skills and time.

A number of strands were established with varying degrees of success:

- Crowdfunding, which was supported by a social media campaign and a prize draw,
- A membership fee for those joining which was flagged during recruitment and social media 'broadcasts' to people keen to join,
- Using AI to pick up nuances and obfuscations from elected party faithful and then sharing these through several social media to become an 'influencer' and paid by advertisers,
- Several donors were sought – people with money and influence who were quite disillusioned with the state of UK politics in general and inequality in particular,

- Several opportunistic events[29] were managed such as book sales, seminars, lectures, long walks and events; the effort was high and the returns low. These occasions did, however, offer additional opportunities for recruitment (see below),
- The website had been constructed to support and encourage donations from people who were interested but not sufficiently committed to actively participate in the movement,
- A Local Growth Fund was set up based on The Bank of Dave. (A Community Bank) which had been established over 20 years ago and full marks to Dave Fishwick for taking on the establishment and winning – and even though he is a Lancastrian (Burnley) a good idea doesn't care where it came from. The point with the Yorkshire version is that it was:
    - Focused on societal money (notes and coins in circulation[30]), not the fiat money generated from thin air (see Appendix 1.3), and
    - Established specifically to support the local community – whether commercial, not for profit or the individuals themselves.

---

[29] Both as a physical presence and on-line (Zoom for example)

[30] There is a broader discussion in 'Yorkshire 2027 – A Strategy for Tomorrow'

<u>Promoting the Cause.</u>

In the early stages of any new venture the message is muted and open to misinterpretation. The approach adopted was to reach out with clear and simple messages (see above) using the following approaches – none too difficult to manage, each relatively easy to focus and collectively quite powerful:

- Traditional geographic print media, e.g. The Yorkshire Post for wide coverage; The Press (&other local titles) for regional coverage,
- Broadcast media which included Radio York, Radio Leeds, Radio Humberside and Coast & County Radio (Scarborough),
- Social media – growing contacts and 'friends' to share the message and gain interest and feedback,
- Our own website – describing, encouraging and verifying broadcasts and communications.
- Yorkshire Agricultural Society etc. – playing to fracking, changes to planning permission and loss of control over (managed) estates,
- Yorkshire Universities and university societies – intelligent, undecided youngsters (Forge Radio is student run for example),
- Womens' Institutes – interested, influential and underestimated,
- Probus magazine etc. – the clubs are autonomous but comprised of retired business people, keen to stay active and involved, and
- Meetup Groups – special interest groups were set up in York, Leeds, Sheffield and Humberside,

<u>Finding Recruits</u>

As well as considering the ways to promote the cause, location was also taken into account and the most appropriate active areas in Yorkshire for media, gatherings and groups were:

- York
- Hull
- Bridlington
- Leeds
- Harrogate
- Sheffield
- Thirsk

There were additional locations to these within driving distance for example Beverley and Driffield are within easy reach of Hull.

The individuals and organisations that were approached and became involved are noted below under <u>Appropriate People types.</u>

The building blocks were in place to establish The Thing, which was charged with influencing politicians' decisions about Yorkshire and also with the option later to become a new social force if that was to become a meaningful option.

Part 4. The Thing From 2024.

The support was now in place for a couple of candidates to stand at the 2024 election; success was expected to be marginal – certainly not as good as the established parties (with all their weaknesses) but better than an individual or independent candidate because people still like to feel part of a group or larger organisation such as a political party.

The name used was *Yorkshire Rising* to reflect a focus on increasing influence & well-being whilst harking back to those who bemoan the passing of the three Ridings.

This was not registered as a party, and the word 'party' was scrupulously omitted from all communications; flying a bit close to the wind? Yes, but better to ask for forgiveness afterwards than ask for permission beforehand and then spend months messing about with cumbersome administration and legal delays.

The aims from the start were, in particular:

- To recognise those particulars that were most important for society, commerce and public services.
- To identify wards which supported The Thing.
- To identify the most cost-effective way to reach out to people.
- To characterise the types of people that would command respect and be trusted.
- To gauge the responses – positive and negative by the major parties to this new approach which was their 'competition'.

Society, Commerce & Public Services.

Society.

Society is the ultimate arbiter – without society we are alone, naked and helpless; with no sense of belonging, purpose or dignity.

In the past we charged elected people working at a distance to represent us and hold our communities together in ways that are meaningful to each of us.

However, the personal materialism of these elected people, adherence to party lines regardless of the situation of their constituents and their pandering to close contacts had, over time, inexorably drained the freedom, equality and sense of identity from us.

The disparate nature of Yorkshire demanded different needs to different sections of society with greater local control of transport in rural areas, law & order in towns and cities and investment in commercial centres.

We needed to get rid of the 'one size fits all' mentality of the established political parties and replace it with direct thinking and action to the smaller defined groups of constituents.

North Yorkshire had tried to establish something similar with Community Network Partnerships but such was the administration and 'points of order' that people had become disheartened with the idea which made little difference on the ground and served to cause an additional hurdle to people joining The Thing as they anticipated a similar pantomime.

The Thing established its own non-political links with societies and 'clusters' bringing people and industry together such that mutual cooperation and support began to take root.

Many initiatives had already been started, the key was to give people the confidence to make fuller use of them; initiatives that included purchasing groups, time banks, local e-networks and regular local meetings – much facilitated through the grey warriors, many of whom were seeking new challenges being retired and determined not to become inactive.

<u>Commerce</u>.

Not only society, but also local commerce had been poorly supported for years, investing on broken promises by Westminster politicians, tolerating poor infrastructure and needing to retrain people due to poor national education.

The Thing established a range of programmes with societies and groups having a vested interest in commerce and brought them together with companies and organisations to begin to realise mutual benefit. This is discussed in more detail elsewhere[31]; this more protracted and pervasive programme that had been instigated also served as an effective recruiting programme.

Coming up to 2027 and beyond saw the start of a programme focusing on particular influential centres; for example not only where industry is

---

[31] *Yorkshire 2027 & <u>Developing Relationships</u> below*

concentrated, which includes Leeds & Bradford and Humberside & Sheffield; but also areas where tourism and agriculture are important including Richmond, Ripon and York.

Other locations, not specifically targeted, joined in including Middlesborough and Scarborough.

Teams were established in these centres to work with Chambers of Commerce, Business Clubs, Accountancies and other interested parties to initiate and maintain programmes of mutual support.

Public Services.

Education, NHS, Police and the Emergency Services are big, bureaucratic and under central control; they were also tied into debilitating PPP contracts (noted elsewhere under World Economic Forum). Their size and established legal commitments put them out of reach of The Thing, such that there were few opportunities for direct intervention.

That said, a number of the issues that could potentially be tackled were identified and flagged so that later, when out of PPP agreements for example, influence would be brought to bear on these bigger issues.

Introducing The Thing.

One indicator was opinion polls carried out on behalf of the main parties and broadcasters. The *national* figures suggested that 45% favoured

Labour, 25% favoured Conservative and 12% favoured the Lib Dems.

Yorkshire however showed a different pattern[32] with the various constituencies quite polarised. Results from the early 2020s, identified constituencies where there was a degree of balance as:

- Thirsk & Malton 38/31 C/L (Con hold)
- Skipton & Ripon 35/33 C/L (Con hold)
- Bridlington & The Wolds 39/36 C/L (Con hold)
- Beverley & Holderness 41/37 L/C (Lab gain)

Other Yorkshire constituencies showed a significant bias to Labour or Conservative with the exception of Harrogate with a strong preference for Lib Dem.

Things had got so bad by 2024 with the Conservatives' unpopularity and a rather wet approach by Labour, that people voted for the 'least worst' not for the best.

The four constituencies noted above were selected as the ones in which to enter candidates under the *Yorkshire Risings* banner. None succeeded in becoming elected but all retained their deposits and created a significant amount of general interest by voters and in the media.

---

[32] https://electionmaps.uk/nowcast

<u>Reaching Out Cost-effectively.</u>

In preparing for the 2027 election[33], experience had shown that newspaper adverts had little traction (partly due to social media being the preferred sources of information) appearances at hustings did little to influence people; both activities took a lot of time (preparing adverts, travelling) or were expensive. Approaches using QR codes and blog/website manifestos had little effect – QR codes seemingly little used in the UK.

The foci of communication were social media, radio/TV broadcasts and newspaper articles (regarded as independent), supported by the free delivery of leaflets by the Post Office, however the cost of the leaflets was substantial and the deliveries were to selected organisations and people. Emphasis was placed on The Thing, not the individual.

Some time was spent giving presentations where the material might be reported and the audience influential or suitable for recruitment, for example to Probus, Chambers of Commerce, Womens' Institute.

Two constituencies were selected where majorities had been quite slim, these being Thirsk & Malton and Beverley & Holderness; constituencies which also benefited The Thing by having established local radio, a strong regional culture and local newspapers specific to the area.

---

[33] This election came early because Westminster was ungovernable due to an insufficient majority and the balance of power being held by the smaller parties.

The messages in all cases were not only for people to vote but also to join The Thing and contribute – whether expertise, time or donations.

The feedback from the targeted communications, whether social media ('friends' referrals), broadcast media or presentations encouraged people to become involved, growing the number of active members.

<u>Appropriate People Types.</u>

In the early stages of becoming established, the types of people needed were those who actually did things – and did things for others, rather than hold endless discussions with several reports.

The over-riding principle was that an altruistic order that could bring the various groups together and work across boundaries would flourish.

Once established, appropriate media and meetings were used to gain additional interest from potentially supportive people and bodies.

Examples included:

<u>Political & Influential People.</u>

- Local Mayors
- Parliamentarians
- County Councillors
- Broadcasters
- Hereditary landowners

Education & Research.

- Local education Authorities
- University Planners & Managers
- Head Teachers
- Standards Officers & Evaluators
- Examination Boards

Healthcare.

- Preventative – gyms etc.
- Diagnostic – surgeries etc.
- Curative
- Recovery, recuperation & rehabilitation
- Supportive – Nursing homes, palliative
- Specialist – addiction, mental health

Law & Order.

- Intelligence
- Prevention
- Catching & charging
- Punishment & rehabilitation
- Control – traffic, events

Societies and people involved in them.

- Cities & suburbs: Sheffield, Middlesborough
- Landowners: commercial recreational, tourist
- Property owners: landlords, pension funds

Financial.

- Investors
- Bankers (including The Bank of Dave)

- Economists
- Advisors

The coming together of these groups whether as special interest, general interest or mutually beneficial is discussed below under <u>Developing Relationships.</u>

The foundations were in place to support growth and recruitment leading from the 2027 election.

<u>Responses By The Major Parties.</u>

In 2024, the major parties were too busy fighting for parliamentary seats to pay much attention to a new organisation in far-away Yorkshire called *The Thing* – Labour had been making empty promises, Conservatives inventing new bribes that would never be realised[34] and the Liberals trying to decide what is was that made them different or desirable.

The Thing was ignored.

---

[34] For example, in mid-2024 inflation miraculously met the government's target (a 'better' set of criteria had been recently identified) and therefore taxation could be reduced – just in time for the election.

Earlier Preparation For 2027.

Following the 2024 election a number of the 'displaced' politicians showed interest in The Thing as a means to get back into power. It was important to continue to exercise a degree of selectivity over who was part of the management team, who was put forward to stand and to recognise those who became part of local councils and ginger groups.

The success of *The Thing* attracted attention from a number of directions with different people beginning to come forward to stand at the 2027 election and a sufficient caucus to bring increasing influence to bear on the media, interested societies and the public in general.

By 2027, sufficient funds had accumulated to hire staff, campaigners and specialists to maintain, and grow, momentum. Even so, additional funds were needed as deposits for the up-coming candidates.

A number of significant changes had happened between 2024 and 2027, some are noted elsewhere[35] and included global currencies losing value, loss of intellectual protection, shoddy overseas supplies and global changes to weather.

Changes to the voting system

Here the focus was on the changes to central government and the relevance of those changes.

---

[35] See *Yorkshire 2027* pg. 12 ff

After 2024, the ruling Labour Party was just short of a working majority and was being supported by the Liberals; the Liberals were unhappy because, again, their numbers in Parliament did not reflect the votes received, there were 25 Liberal MPs, approximately 4% of those elected, yet their proportion of the votes indicated they should have about 14% of seats – 90 in all.

On one particularly contentious vote, the Liberals threatened to vote with the Conservatives unless a system of Proportional Representation (PR) was introduced.

This was supported by the Greens and others who were disaffected that their proportion of votes did not provide an appropriate level of representation.

Proportional Representation has been used by roughly half the countries around the world (90 out of 195).

As an approximate calculation in 2019 there were just short of 31m votes cast for 650 seats. In order to be given a single seat, an individual would need to poll just short of 50,000 votes nationally.

This is twice the number of votes given to Yorkshire candidates in the 2019 election and under PR, would not have been considered an adequate result to get an MP elected. A significant campaign was launched, making the most of available technology.

As an aside, a number of other regions had noticed *The Thing* and were working along similar lines to get a better deal from Westminster.

<u>The Influences Of Technology.</u>

The incredible developments in technology since 2024 delivered, amongst other things, Artificial Intelligence (AI) capable of mimicking, modifying or manufacturing just about any existing material, input or message.

Up to 2024, most of the use of this technology (machine intelligence) was its use in inputting maximum user data for the purpose of selling targeted advertising[36], later the circle was completed and technology could be deployed to develop its own outputs as well as colleting disparate inputs.

By 2026, AI was still a loose cannon despite innumerable papers, cross-discipline meetings and various summits; the lack of regulation (paradoxically also held back by the *Precautionary Principle*[37]) was no doubt due to debate being more news-worthy than results; and, self-interest sitting at the top of everyone's agenda.

Needless to say, AI was being used both positively and negatively; in politics, to try to gain favour for prospective candidates and to undermine competition. To overcome the lack of trust in social media and political rhetoric, *The Thing* was very deliberate in the choice of technology deployed in 2027 to communicate its message.

The way technology was used was very selective:

---

[36] Please see *The Age of Surveillance Capitalism* by Shoshana Zuboff pg. 95ff. Published 2019.

[37] For a more complete discussion, please see *Climate Uncertainty and Risk* by Judith Curry pg.167.

- AI to gain data and analyse needs and trends; <u>but</u> <u>not</u> to deliver messaging.
- Facebook and other social media to deliver information and messages.
- A website in which all communication was filed, cross-referenced, verified and made publicly available.

All of the above was carefully controlled by a small number of people who had a significant degree of competence in these fields, including retired teachers, interested geeks and volunteer technologists.

<u>Working To Elect MPs in 2027.</u>

As noted elsewhere[38] organisations were forming clusters and a few were gaining a degree of prominence, particularly in Sheffield, Leeds and Hull; only Hull had been one of the key seats in 2024 and, being a bit isolated, Hull and surrounding wards were able to influence without too much interference from Westminster and the established parties feeling under threat.

The Thing started to work with these clusters, and Hull in particular, to strengthen them and, in the process gain members, influence and support.

Specific targets were set to deliver MPs specific to Yorkshire in the 2027 election. These targets included:

- A 'fighting fund' of £50,000 to support each candidate throughout Yorkshire (every vote

---

[38] *Yorkshire 2027* and also at *Clustering* below

counts) to the tune of £500 for their deposits and an additional £500 for print costs[39], candidates were at liberty to boost this amount from personal funds if they saw fit to do so.

- At least four volunteers from each cluster with the skills and expertise to support the wider cause.
- Monthly decision-making meetings, growing in numbers as the programme progressed; meetings drawing together key players from each cluster in order to co-ordinate activity.
- Monthly meetings in the clusters to plan and deliver Members of Parliament to support their particular interests (which varied from cluster to cluster).

All the time supported by AI, focused on the particular cluster to analyse and identify core priorities that had significant importance to that electorate – a number of centres had households, facilities and services already interlinked by cable which supported data gathering and interpretation.

<u>Publicity.</u>

As noted above, the campaign had demanded a broadcast approach, individual presentations were very time-consuming and avoided unless a particular group was very influential and pervasive, or the event was being reported in the press, radio or TV.

The campaign started towards the end of 2025 when the dust from the election had settled and the

---

[39] The Post Office delivered a leaflet free to each household in the ward.

various main parties had begun to show their inability to deal with national economics, AI, Infrastructure investment, education and the NHS.

Discontent was growing and would continue to do so for the next two years; a strategy was developed that identified the issues that mattered in the particular Cluster Wards and working solutions were offered to address those issues.

Similar projects were started across Yorkshire which recognised government shortcomings and created workable solutions, consistent with national economics, that could be applied locally.

Communication included:

- Local radio, which often struggles to fill air time accepted a series of 15 minute slots interviewing a knowledgeable individual. Such a series of programmes can be reasonably easy realised; for example BBC local radio ran 12 quarter-hour slots discussing economics on Thursdays starting at 11:45 from just a phone call to that particular radio station.
- Pithy posts on Facebook and other social media; detailing simple statements of the issue, solutions and with a reference to a more detailed analysis on the website.
- Articles in various publications with stories about successes and benefits delivered

In all cases, recruitment was actively encouraged, whether individual membership, commercial sponsorship or group involvement. In return for financial support, each contributor got regular updates, invitations to get-togethers and free coaching from volunteers in topics relevant to them, for example financial advice for individuals, marketing workshops for commercial sponsors and access to AI analyses for groups.

Again targets were set, which were to have achieved over three years:

- For the County, 2,000 individuals at £25.00 per annum.
- For each of three Ridings, 25 commercial sponsors at £500.00 per annum (equivalent to less than one day's consultancy/training).
- 45 Member Regional Groups of 50 people, £15.00 per member (a £10.00 per person encouragement for groups to form).

25% was gained in year one, 70% by the end of year 2 and the target reached immediately before the 2027 election.

The income figures involved came out at:

March 2025	£ 30,313
March 2026	£ 84,875
March 2027	£ 121,250

Whilst the income figures look quite good (and do not include crowdfunding and other income generating opportunities) there are also overheads; and, in particular, a technologist who was on a wage of £20,000 a year plus a bonus of 8% of all income, however generated, above £50,000.

Staff costs were based on several part-timers and volunteers estimated as full-time equivalents at £18,500 per annum (based on minimum wage). The growth in headcount from 2024 was:

2025 – all volunteers,

2026 – 1 full time equivalent,
2027 – 2 full time equivalents (election support),
Employers NI was taken as 10% of payroll.

£5,000 was the annual rental of office space in the HUB.

By the 2027 election The Thing had covered its costs, contributed £1,000 per ward and after the election was still sufficiently solvent to continue growth and development.

<u>The 2027 Election Results.</u>

54 candidates were sponsored and supported by a range of media orchestrated by The Thing's permanent technician with issues relating to ward-specific issues and options to address these issues with the implications for the voters in each ward.

5 of the seats gained in excess of 5,000 votes per Yorkshire candidate (those constituencies unsure how to vote).

10 seats gained 1,500 votes per candidate and the rest collected an average of 450 votes per candidate.

The final tally was just short of 60,000 votes in total – sufficient under the new Proportional Representation model for one candidate to be elected to Westminster as an MP.

As of 2028, the elected MP set about marshalling Yorkshire behind a programme of change and improvement, supported by:
- Residual funds from donations etc.,
- Office expenses paid by Westminster to its MPs,
- Prospective candidates who lost in the election,

- The established team of volunteers,
- Dedicated staff, and
- Unexpectedly seconded staff.

The unexpectedly seconded staff were provided by the various councils and other public bodies, keen to know what was going on and what might challenge their power base.

There was now enough support to engage people across the County with the benefit that the elected MP did not belong to any of the major parties, was of a personality driven by a temperament of cooperation, and worked to deliver some real benefit supported by the regional mayors, councils and those not elected in the 2027 election. But more of that later.

The time was right in 2028, with The Thing having the staff and the funds to launch a dedicated programme, that reached out across Yorkshire, to link groups and people, encourage cooperative working and begin to invest in the County where Westminster had singularly failed over decades.

<u>Clustering.</u>

<u>Developing Relationships.</u>

In addition to socialising events such as dinners, presentations, visits and the like, two formats were used to bring people together, formats which had been proven to work over decades, these being the RSA and the CMI's MRG.

The RSA (Royal Society of Arts[40]) was founded over 250 years ago to bring people of all interests together in an informal and neutral setting to share ideas, learn and begin to understand the pressures placed on other people and which may, or may not, provide opportunities or threats; for example, money laundering regulations & their enforcement may impact transfer pricing by an exporter.

CMI (The Chartered Management Institute) established a series of more formal forums – Their MRGs (Management Research Groups) which met over dinner and comprised Managing Partners, Company Directors and senior people from the public sector. Members of the Management Institute with a novel experience or a problem to solve put their names forward to visit a Group where the Members' would learn from the others' experience or offer suggestions to overcome the problem – sharing best practice, learning & improving.

---

[40] More fully *The Royal Society of Arts, Manufactures and Commerce*. Manufactures & Commerce seem to have been forgotten recently.

Building Relationships.

Beneficial relationships were encouraged, developed and strengthened by making appropriate use of the above formats – the informal dinners, informal learning and formal groups including:
* Cooperation within similar Groups.
* Cooperation between different Groups.
* Cooperation between multiple Groups.
* Joint Group discussions.

Similar Groups.

These included:
* Business-to-business, for example accountants (ICAEW), farmers (NFU) and distribution (RHA[41]).
* Not-For Profit organisations such as charities and local libraries.

Disparate Groups.

More common were associations between complimentary organisations which may be:
* For profit such as manufacturer/distributor or finance/IT.
* Not for profit where there is a common interest such as councils and service providers.

---

[41] Institute of Chartered Accountants in England & Wales, National Farmers' Union and the Road Haulage Association

Multiple Groups.

Such groups were encouraged by organisations such as:

- The ISBE – The Institute for Small Business and Entrepreneurship (registered in Barnsley) which draws together small business, research and support.
- Chambers of Commerce which are open to local businesses, providing a social space with occasional presentations & points of interest.

Joint Group Discussions.

Such discussions were organised by all of the Groups noted above and normally revolved around something of mutual interest such as:

- Impending legislation.
- Financial trends.
- Education & Apprenticeships.

All of these groups built relationships which could be developed for mutual benefit – whether increased sales, reduced overheads or shared resources.

The Thing encouraged, developed and chaired events that involved the scenarios described above where everyone involved benefited and Yorkshire, as a whole, enjoyed greater prosperity.

Benefits Of The Relationships.

How the events were managed is discussed in some detail later; below is a list of some examples:

Similar Groups.

RSA Format
- Ideas to developed and improved own business.
- Greater cooperation and improved efficiencies.

MRG Format
- Specific issues resolved.
- Shared suppliers, referred markets.

Different Groups.

RSA Format
- Transfer of ideas/new ways of working.
- Market opportunities.

MRG Format
- Improved (non-traditional) ways of working.
- Non-competitive shared distribution.

Multiple Groups.

RSA Format
- Opportunistic new contacts identified.
- Potential opportunities to progress identified.

MRG Format
- Clearer business focus.
- New ways to overcome constraints.

Joint Group Discussions.

RSA Format
- Updates to current thinking.
- Appreciate constraints on others (e.g. supply).

MRG Format
- Priorities better contextualised.
- Shared management approaches.

<u>Developing A Greater Presence.</u>

Details from all the above events were captured to be used as material for advertising, recruitment and growing credibility. SOME OF The means of developing the greater presence are noted below.

<u>Reports,</u> detailing the various group discussions, conclusions, opportunities and benefits that arose. These reports were then posted to the website and sent as complimentary copies to existing members, potential new Members and selected libraries.

<u>Website</u> tailored to Members' needs, with sound analytics (e.g. frequency of page views), analytics of visitor profiles to put people together into new groups and verification of all material posted on social media to underscore credibility.

<u>Traditional media</u> releases through local newspapers as well as County-wide newspapers about what The Thing is delivering for Yorkshire. This involved cultivating good relationships, providing articles and occasional advertorials. Additionally, spots on local radio who often need to fill odd slots.

<u>Social Media</u> using verified material to keep Members and Members' contacts up to speed with the various groups and outputs from The Thing that are influencing how politics is being managed around the County.

Published Articles which may come from any of the Members, Groups or other interested parties; these were posted to the same recipients as the Reports with addition of topic journals where appropriate.

Think Tanks were established within Groups and between Members where reports from meetings, website feedback or issues emerged. These think tanks involved those specialists who were Members coming together to prepare a 'Thought Paper' to circulate, generate feedback and increase involvement in The Thing.

Podcasts were posted on the website with Members and prospective Members alerted through e-mail or social media – again, to increase interest and involvement.

As noted above The resulting growth in interest and Membership led to a number of people ambitious to represent and support Yorkshire Equality and one of those people had become an MP due to a change to Proportional Representation.

The energy after the 2027 election was to maximise political influence to benefit the County and prepare the way for greater political representation.

Part 5. Integration Delivery & Growth.

Becoming Increasingly Political.

The 2027[42] election demonstrated that people had the will to rise and flourish, take control and oversee the various communities that make up Yorkshire society; give back to the people the rightful dignity to once again feel proud of their particular mind-set and the title *Northerners*.

Given new MPs, and their support provided (ironically) by Westminster, offices were established with the aim of correcting some of the inadequacies of 2024-27, in particular inadequacies in:

- Political representation in Society.
- Investment in infrastructure.
- Encouragement for Commerce and Innovation.

And to begin to develop alternative forms of finance for local investment.

Support For Society.

The key issues that were addressed included:

- Bringing political decision-making closer to home,
- Constructive use of Artificial Intelligence,
- Efficiency in local politics (reduced bureaucracy),
- Public service delivery, and
- Housing – including social housing.

---

[42] Called early because of Labour's slim majority and the balance of power with the Liberals making meaningful governance all but impossible.

<u>Political Decision-Making.</u>

By 2027, the political cycle[43] had turned from one of reporting and recording but no action to one where action was needed – and quite urgently, to cope with the very rapidly changing world order where levers of government were getting progressively gummed up.

For over 3 decades government had progressively centralised power, relied upon consultancies and preserved the state described elsewhere as "Maintain the status quo, and work from a nice address"[44] this push for centralisation had led to paralysis through overload and one of the main solutions had been to abandon decision-making to the big consultancies, thereby 'hollowing out' governments which, in turn, had led to lost experience and minimal evolution in terms of staff capabilities.

Senior politicians had been open to this change because it hid a lot of their poor decisions, or lack of decisions, and opened the door to someone else to blame.

Over the last four years *The Yorkshire Thing* had created an efficient structure, adopted a decision-making process using AI based on local need and by becoming increasingly involved in the clusters

---

[43] See Yorkshire 2027 pg.10 ff.

[44] For an excellent and thorough study of government's tinkering at the edges, avoiding meaningful decisions and lack of any significant purpose or progress please see Dick Stroud's book *The Secondary Mod* ISBN 978-0995657724.

forming in the major centres of population and commerce was now developing significant experience and expertise.

The lead was the MP supported by The Thing elected in 2024 who had received the most votes, and making up the MP's team were the volunteers, staff and those who had been sufficiently motivated to stand at election, all working together to connect and support the various groups.

Worth repeating here is the sentiment expressed by Wilson & Wilson.

Selfishness beats altruism within groups. Altruistic groups [parties] beat selfish groups. Everything else is commentary.

Usage Of Artificial Intelligence (AI).

As noted above (*Need For A New Party*) There had been a great many benefits from the development and deployment of AI, from improved medication to handling dangerous situations; however, being global, it was too big, too complex and too pervasive to be managed by Yorkshire alone, we needed to accept whatever controls were imposed whilst taking maximum advantage of the technology of the day.

Despite all the good stuff there are bad actors who have used AI to disrupt society, gain power to themselves and actually use it as a weapon of war impacting elections, finance[45] and communications.

---

[45] Please see also *Currency Wars* by James Rickards which predicted financial warfare back in 2012 but did

The impact has been to undermine national fiat currencies, investments and electronic transactions[46] yet the government was caught asleep at the wheel noy knowing which way to turn or what to do.

After the 2024 build-up and the 2027 election win, the reach and influence of *The Yorkshire Thing* covered some of the more densely populated areas of the County and in particular the centres of influence including Hull, Middlesborough, Leeds, Sheffield and York.

These areas commanded a great deal of influence by dint of concentrated population and as centres of industry; consequently, there was a tendency for them to be favoured for investment.

A great many factors come into play with investment, some are plain for example where a road or a building is in need of repair, some less obvious such as education and training needs and some subject to the rhetoric or position of the individual or group seeking investment. AI had been embraced and developed to a point where a balanced, logical and dispassionate analysis could be made on behalf of the County as a whole, leading to more equitable investment and greater social cohesion.

<u>Efficiency In Local Politics.</u>

In commerce, there is a general 'rule-of-thumb' that the cost of an organisation's administration

---

not anticipate the speed with which AI could ramp up the aggression and hack national and personal accounts.

[46] Please see Appendix 1.

should be between 16% and 25% of turnover. Below that figure there is a risk of being ripped-off; above that figure, management can be considered to have lost sight of their objective[47].

As noted earlier, government focuses on policies which can change at a whim, whilst business runs on objectives which derive from the purpose of the organisation and are permanent. Objectives drive strategy and direct any modification of tactics when external circumstances change.

A clear objective has already been articulated for The Thing so the level of bureaucracy can be managed to an appropriate level.

Unlike a particular government organisation, where one branch was established by selected professionals with 32% administration – which was pretty good for a government body. But after five years with Parliamentarians showing increasing interest and managers lacking the intertesticular fortitude to brush them off admin had grown to 82% of the funds directed through this particular office and the number of parameters reported to Westminster had grown spectacularly.

It was recognised that The Thing needed a greater level of bureaucracy than commerce and the cost of administration was capped at 40%.

---

[47] "Having lost sight of our objective, we redoubled our efforts" Ascribed to Walt Kelly and also Igor Ansoff.

<u>Public Service Delivery.</u>

<u>Introduction.</u>

Over time, governments both national and local have been persuaded by consultancies that they can be more efficient by sub-contracting services, much as PPP was 'sold' as beneficial. Looking back this has only been beneficial to the banks, politicians and big conglomerates, supported and coordinated through the World Economic Forum (WEF).

Wikipedia's entry concerning the WEF concludes "[WEF has] … received criticism over the years, including the organization's corporate capture of global and democratic institutions, its institutional whitewashing initiatives, the public cost of security, the organization's tax-exempt status, unclear decision processes and membership criteria, a lack of financial transparency, and the environmental footprint of its annual meetings."

The lack of transparency is evident in the way consultancies have advised on the structure of budgets and a dictum that "If it's not spent by the year end you won't get it next year." One ex-councillor bought five unnecessary photocopiers one year end to spend up to budget, another example is a London council which did an exercise on its budget lines where permanent staff had one budget line, while agency staff had a second budget line, and because of the strict rules budgets could only be used for the staff profiles they represented.

The additional cost in agency staff was 2.4 times that of employed staff; so it would have been possible to more than halve the wage bill through direct employment. It was surmised that an already weakened management lacked the capacity to make decisions that might be contentious – like firing incompetent staff when agency workers were easily replaced and they could always move to another council and be incompetent there.

Additional unnecessary costs are incurred in employing expensive consultancies when decisions and projects could be managed in-house "Employees in [big[48]] business and government are becoming frustrated with being reduced to consultancy contract managers …"[49] – perhaps to avoid being blamed for something?

<u>Taking Public Service delivery back in-house.</u>

The Thing's earlier joiners were mostly from commercial backgrounds, either as volunteers or retired – people who were used to making decisions. They used this experience along with the elected MPs to bring pressure to bear on councils, training personnel and to challenge the various consultancies and agencies.

Eventually, one council did take a more 'relaxed' approach to budgeting and a firmer approach to staff.

Significant sums were released from council budgets some of which could now be used for local

---

[48] My addition.
[49] *The Big Con* Mazzucato & Collington Pg.253

social programmes which included sports halls, swimming pools, theatres and galleries.

Housing & Social Housing.

The notional value of property has grown at a much faster rate than inflation which has been reflected in rents rising above inflation and property-owners reaping the rewards. Tenants, now increasingly hard up were supported by ever greater cost of living allowances.

This is an interesting merry-go-round where the wealthy elite screw the disadvantaged who, in turn are propped up by public money through allowances so the disadvantaged can pay the higher rents with public money that finds its way into the pockets of the elite. The privileged supporting the privileged by recycling public money.

Councils were encouraged to significantly increase costs, community charges and penalties on vacant property, land banks, brown-field sites and holiday homes in order to release land and properties for builders and developers to create social housing. Additionally, council housing that had been (expensively) sub-contracted to friends and cronies was taken back into public ownership.

Since 2027, staff in public office were trained in property management ready for the exorbitant PPP arrangements not being renewed.

The 2032 Election

In the five years since the 2027 election The Thing had been steadily developing, growing in membership, becoming increasingly influential and, most importantly, seen locally to be more relevant than political parties.

The officers of The Thing had jobs that mirror the structural requirements to establish a new political party; in 2028 the decision was made to incorporate *The Yorkshire Rising Party* as a political entity with the people standing for election in 2032 selected from members of The Thing by its officers, people whose driver was the County and not personal gain.

The Yorkshire Rising Party was managed as a separate entity because the goal was to develop a greater presence in Westminster which could influence investment in the County whilst The Thing was establishing a greater presence in the County and working to influence Westminster.

The two functions were complimentary, but to work had to be managed separately due to different missions and purpose.

The influence of The Thing had grown and its support for The Yorkshire Rising Party was recognised across the County and by the media, such that when the election came about the 54 seats generated enough proportional votes to put six of the candidates into Westminster.

More important though, for Yorkshire, was The Thing and that remained the focus despite political success.

Encouraging Commerce & Innovation.

Meanwhile back in Yorkshire, commerce and innovation pervade all aspects of life by providing goods & services – adding value to raw ingredients; and, through wages, adding value to peoples' lives.

Progressively, this simple arrangement has been subverted by outsourcing to the BRICK[50] countries where wage rates are low and staff welfare might be minimal, thereby increasing margins that go to benefit shareholders at the expense of the workforce.

Government support for commerce has been minimal, allowing take-overs that repatriate profits, the hollowing-out of national brands and allowing companies to close factories that have been the envy of the world, such as high-end steelworks.

Consultancies had focused commerce on 'added shareholder value' to the detriment of the workforce and even the organisations' own markets[51]. Most, if not all, of this has been to support the major corporates – many of which are a part of, or contribute to, the pretty much discredited World Economic Forum (see above) promoting riches for the already rich.

Historically, a long time ago, there was a relationship between government and industry where government invested in industry and industry paid corporation tax.

---

[50] Brazil, Russia, India, China, Korea.
[51] Please see *Value – The Four Cornerstones of Corporate Finance* by McKinsey.

The corporation tax, along with income tax, provided the funds to invest back in society, thereby enriching the lives of the local people.

However, since the deregulation of the banks (with tax 'advice' from the consultancies provided simultaneously to government collecting tax and the rich paying it) an amazing raft of legal tax avoidance[52] measures have come into law such that the tax paid by the conglomerates is pitiful, for example some years ago, the statistic was forwarded that 50% of UK employment was with the conglomerates, 50% with SMEs[53] yet the total corporation tax paid in the UK was 8% from the conglomerates, 92% from the SMEs!

An additional spanner in the works has been the banks who are risk averse outside their own sphere of interest; but inside their own sphere huge risks have been taken with investments (See Appendix 1.3), possibly because it's not their money and scrutiny is minimal; but, as an SME trying to get bank funding for a new development or to enter a new market and you hit a brick wall. A number of profitable products developed in the UK had to go abroad for funding including Dyson and Brompton bikes, and have flourished, at this country's expense!

Despite this, there is still an appetite for development amongst SME and individuals; this is where support was mainly directed.

---

[52] Tax avoidance is legal, tax evasion (e.g. the 'black economy') is not and is punishable.

[53] Small & Medium-sized Enterprises.

<u>Support For New Developments.</u>

The Thing's support provided to the SMEs centred on disciplines normally outside their normal sphere of activity and included:

- Application of emerging technology,
- Marketing research,
- Management skills & strategy,
- Intellectual protection,
- Sales support,
- Access to finance,

<u>Application of emerging technology.</u>

The Thing had deliberately invested in emerging technology (e.g. AI) and in people with the skills to manage it. The power of the system is such that it was made available to SMEs and (verified?) entrepreneurs on a library-type basis – much as on-line searches were provided by libraries in the late 1980s where help was provided in developing appropriate phrasing for the questions to get usable answers.

Many new ventures and start-ups don't have the necessary experience or analytical skills to establish a meaningful research programme. Support people had these skills and coached the new ventures through the various processes to ensure that in future new ventures had the skills to expand and diversify successfully.

The people using the AI service were registered with The Thing to ensure probity and to control usage; in addition, usage carried a fee which contributed to running costs and also towards investment in other new ventures.

Management Skills & Strategy.

Two lines of support were provided:
- Coaching & mentoring,
- Formal teaching and qualifications.

Many of the volunteer support team had been managers and were now retired, looking to maintain an interest in business and provided support and encouragement for new businesses – targeted to where those businesses had gaps in experience, whether finance, marketing or personnel. Bridging these gaps provided the confidence to move forward surely and effectively.

In addition to coaching and mentoring, formal qualifications were provided through organisations such as the Chartered Management Institute (CMI) or The Institute of Leadership & Management (ILM).

For a modest fee Members were, naturally, allowed to attend courses even if not sitting the formal assessment.

Intellectual Protection.

Protecting an idea is a minefield, whether a patent, a trademark or a copyright; proving infringement is a playground for lawyers and the big firms can play the game of running the complainant out of money. An additional concern is that not all countries have signed up to mutually uphold each others' citizens rights.

A number of Members were, or had been, lawyers and could offer advice about whether to protect or not, and how to manage the right sort of protection.

Advice was also available about how to research whether an idea was already protected which would avoid future problems.

Sales Support.

Whether a new product into an existing market or an existing product into a new market the likelihood is that different sales tactics will be required. These tactics may be direct contact – such as social media seeking to influence contacts' contacts (or in the old days tele-marketing) or may be indirect through advertorial for example.

Each case will be different depending on the product, the benefits it delivers, the most appropriate customer type and even the geography or local regulations.

As with other help, support was made available for a small fee.

Access to Finance.

As noted above, the traditional High Street banks have historically been very poor at advancing funds for new ventures (at reasonable rates of interest) and where institutions or specialist arms of banks have advanced venture money the rates of interest have been prohibitive (36% p.a. was not unusual).

The various fees for Members' support, and also the Membership subs were banked to be made available for local investment in innovation.

Additionally, as The Thing had grown and demonstrated credibility a number of wealthy people and philanthropists were keen to become associated and support what was seen as a growing and locally beneficial organisation, rather like 'Theatre Angels'.

These monies, plus grants, donations and crowd-funding for example were managed through a copy-cat 'Bank of Dave' which drew together the various sources of funding and support under one roof.

After running costs, money was made available for investment in *approved* developments and innovations. Interest was charged at an agreed proportion of the equity of the venture, not as a percentage, over a fixed number of years; at the end of which point the principal was repaid. This had the advantages that the venture was not hamstrung during its early years and The Thing was incentivised to provide support with returns from successful ventures exceeding the notional interest in later years – offsetting any less successful investments. This is discussed in more detail below.

A New Finance & Investment Model.

<u>Trashing The Currency.</u>

After 2024 when many countries, as well as the UK, had held elections and the various promises made to try to gain votes were being called in; treasuries were running out of money and at the same time there had been a loss of confidence in the banking system with high interest, inflation, devaluation, investments failing, increasing poverty, higher rents and 'austerity' shown to be a sham. Other examples appear in the narrative below.

Local 'work-arounds were coming into being, whether time banks or barter systems; some well controlled, some based on favours. The advantage of The Thing was that the development of a Hub to give focus to individuals, organisations and societies allowed these various work-arounds to be brought to a common base and start to tackle the loss of confidence in traditional money and those who managed it.

An office had been established in York with branch offices in Hull, Sheffield and Leeds.

<u>The Importance of Cooperation.</u>

By 2027 we had learned how to create wealth through cooperation with the template migrating across Yorkshire and with significant interest from the wider North, pretty much a line drawn between the Mersey and the Humber to the south and Hadrian's Wall to the north.

We had also learned that it was sheer folly to rely on London-based political initiatives – from the regeneration schemes of Thatcher's government through Gove's delusional Northern Powerhouse to the ludicrous attempts at 'levelling up'; and, that to get anywhere we had to do things ourselves.

Escalating costs.

Not only was confidence waning for banks but also government had seen money as the nostrum that cured all problems; for example additional incremental costs are incurred whenever there is an operational problem (waiting times, bin emptying, delays to surgical operations) when, instead of better managing the situation, the centralised government has simply thrown more money at it – not their money but public money[54]; little changes, but costs escalate – and yet, they boast about how much has been spent when they should be ashamed.

Couple this with a remark by an MP some time in the 1970s (source lost) who noted to an interviewer "but of course, dear boy; politics is an inherently wasteful process" – wasted on duck houses, chandeliers, moat cleaning and superfluous staff.

Government shortfall is made up by *quantitative easing* (basically, a Ponzi scheme and depends on inflation to pay the interest) which pumps yet more fiat money into the economy, something not available to the rest of us with rents and mortgages.

––––––––––––––––––––––––––––

[54] It's always been easier to spend someone else's money than your own.

As an aside, many MPs[55] own property to rent, where rental is based on a fraction of the market value of the property (around 15%).

A historical perspective in a local free magazine in 2023 compared house prices then with 50 years earlier and stated that in 1973 the average price of a property was £8,144 which, inflated at the same rate as the economy and related to 2023 prices, equated to £92,000.

However, in 2023 the average property price was £296,000 – about three times as much and even if the data was not verified to academic standards, the message is the same. Those with money getting richer, the poor increasingly disadvantaged.

<u>Trashing The Economy.</u>

Thatcher deregulated the banks in 1986 but it took another ten years until Blair was Prime Minister (1996) for the rate of the price increase of property to grow well above inflation and wages, providing an increasing income stream for the banks and the privileged through the interest paid on inflated loans.

Neither should we forget that the bubble bursting in 2008, which was as a result of securitised(?) loans based on fractional reserve banking taken out against price-inflated properties, with minimum security.

---

[55] July 2021, Channel4.com [paraphrase] Almost a fifth of all MPs are landlords, owning houses, flats, farms, holiday cottages and shops.

It's hard to imagine a more frail, irresponsible and paper-thin way to manage other peoples' money – yet still it continued unchecked by those charged with supporting the people and pretending to regulate the money-laundering crooks.

This nonsensical form of economics and management served little purpose other than to drain money from the economy, disadvantage the already disadvantaged and support the privileged elite, a situation that would not be tolerated in any properly managed medium-sized competitive organisation, yet we tolerate it in central government.

The Yorkshire Thing established a York office and branch network staffed by people with a commercial outlook and prepared to make qualified mistakes (and then learn) whilst working to influence and support local government in the quest for improvement where much of the sub-contracted delivery and decision-making was returned to councils and managed internally; the money saved was then invested in answering local needs.

In summary, this operational restructuring did not add any costs to local authorities and other public sector bodies. What it did was provide a model for local authorities to copy which allowed them to get a greater level of investment into the County from the funding provided by Westminster.

The influence that *The Yorkshire Thing* could bring to bear on how the County was supported had begun to grow, aided by the judicious use of Artificial Intelligence.

<u>Recovering the Economy.</u>

Drawing on the experiences, skills and expertise already demonstrated elsewhere in the UK by:

- Time banks (noted earlier),
- The Bank of Dave,
- Local currencies and
- Preston[56].

New ways of working and paying were becoming established and managed, not only locally but as a Yorkshire-wide cooperative.

<u>Time Banks.</u>

The options of local time banks and groups of people cooperating had been developing for some time. In Yorkshire, starting in Hull, with centres later becoming established in the major conurbations and some of the villages; although, in fairness, this had been customary in many rural areas for centuries.

Some of these time banks, but not many, had amalgamated to manage larger tasks and projects but the network has remained fragmented despite the efforts of organisations committed to improve the social fabric as the value of money declined.

The Thing's website had been developed and expanded by the inclusion of AI to recognise where support was needed and who could best deliver that support. It identified where time banks could best be set up locally – or, for bigger projects, alert others in the County.

---

[56] *Paint Your Town Red* Brown & Jones

Time had, effectively, become a currency, managed centrally with credits and debits that were transferrable between centres.

Needless to say, this could not be taxed – but then, neither could it be spent – any more than doing a favour for a neighbour.

There was, however a nominal charge of £1.00 per entry for local connections and £5.00 for connections between centres – but with no guarantee of a connection, it was up to someone with the skills to 'go fishing'. Despite the lack of targeting, modest sums were raised for The Thing whilst saving constituents significant sums that off-set the reductions in earnings caused by poor management by central government.

<u>Alternative Banking.</u>

The most tangible element of someone's wealth is money – whether hard cash or fiat money; hard cash is about 3% of money, fiat money is the rest – an imaginary source of wealth underpinned by belief[57], this fiat money has driven investment bubbles and since 2026 Return On Investment (ROI) had hardened, such that and many people in Yorkshire (and elsewhere for that matter) had been disadvantaged as support for social services had been continually reduced – as typified by reductions in school bus services with some pupils having to change schools or parents move house.

---

[57] Interestingly, in 1964 America changed it's banknotes from *Payable in silver* to *In God we trust.*

Personal care had declined to a point where the average level of personal care was 6¼ hours <u>per annum</u>.[58] per eligible person. All to ensure a return on investment; when surely, people and society are more important than imaginary money.

John Maynard Keynes longed for a day when economists were no longer arch-theorists but instead 'rather like dentists', consulted to solve everyday problems and give straightforward advice. Back in 2025, we thought that day was arriving due to the pressure on governance by an increasingly resolute society, but not so.

Back in 1992, a director of the Midland Bank (as was) told me he was unsure whether the High Street branches were an asset or a liability. By 2026, in their continual drive for profit the banks had removed just about all personal contact with customers, closed branches, moved banking on-line and those High Street branches that remained have been furnished with terminals and a couple of staff to show you how to use them. The personal touch, reassurance and quick advice we had valued so much from the established banks was gone for ever and needed to be put back by different means.

The different means started to be established in a serious manner in 2025 with a Yorkshire based copy of the 'Bank of Dave' and introduction of local currencies; nothing new, just a greater breadth of financial instruments.

---

[58] North Yorkshire leaflet 88236 01/23 justifying the new council and likely savings set up in April 1st 2023

In 2011 Dave Fishwick set up Burnley Savings & Loans Ltd. (The Bank of Dave) after a great deal of resistance and the not unexpected dog-in-a-manger defiance from the establishment of privilege and position – but he succeeded; and offered his experience to those wanting to emulate his success.

This form of banking is societal money only; there is no casino investment, fiat money or ludicrously high fractional reserve.

It works for the community, in the community. An advantage is that local commercial organisations can buy bank equity as a means to reduce declared profit (and also declared taxable surplus).

After three years getting properly established, the Yorkshire version of The Bank of Dave, now re-named *The Restoration Bank* was in a position to put venture capital into start-ups, small businesses and even society – investing by any other name, but not gambling.

As noted above, the venture/investment fund is repaid from the increasing equity value of the organisations taking the investments.

The dividends from this venture fund were channelled into developing The Thing, charities and social causes (some of which could also claim tax relief as *Gift Aid* !).

Establishing such a bank, using one of the vacant big-bank premises opened the way to centralise the time banks and also as a centre to develop a new community currency.

<u>A New Local Currency.</u>

Some thirty years ago, the concept of local UK currencies was established in Totnes and soon afterwards similar local currencies became established in Lewes, Stroud and Brixton.

Those currencies have stayed local and are based on the value of sterling, usually exchanged at parity.

Their benefit is that they keep money circulating in the particular region by people buying mainly local goods and services in preference to distant suppliers(like the trade tokens of 250 years ago).

The problem was that as the value of sterling continued to fall as progressive bubbles burst, the local currencies fell with it. This could be addressed by a lesson from German history.

The hyperinflation of the Reichsmark had trashed the German economy by 1932; the Rentenmark was created as a new currency by the government (not the banks!) and was based on the value of the country per se[59].

People argued then that as a non-convertible currency it could not be used for business, tourism or buying from down the supply chain. The solution was the same as with any other non-convertible currency – create things and export them selling into a convertible currency and then use that overseas currency to buy more stuff to add value to.

---

[59] After only a few months the banks bought up the Rentenmark and issued the Deutschmark which remained the currency until the Euro was adopted. The Rentenmark remained accepted currency until about 1943.

The value of Yorkshire had been established elsewhere and formed the basis for the new currency.

This conferred a number of benefits:
- Not linked to Sterling,
- Value appreciates if productivity increases,
- Benefits are realised locally.

As noted above, historically money had been shifted from those who needed it to those already wealthy, waves of quantitative easing had made up any shortfall, effectively devaluing the currency and making it increasingly expensive to import raw materials for the SME (big firms still outsourced to China etc.).

Local currency encouraged local sourcing which was encouraged and selling into alternative more stable currencies overcame the incremental degradation of Sterling.

Initially linking the value of Yorkshire to the new currency[60] at parity with Sterling gave a base-line from which to manage the County's finances.

The metric used to value the currency was the County's Gross Domestic Product (GDP) per employed person – in much the same way as used by the UK government.

Consequently, as Yorkshire's added-value increases so does the GDP and with it the value of the currency; conversely, if GDP declines, the value of the currency also declines.

---

[60] Designated the *Yorkshire Rose* ¥

This decoupling from Sterling was a strong incentive to drive productivity and living standards.

Once we had learned how to create wealth we learned how to integrate the various options (time banks, barter and local currency) and manage the whole in a way that benefitted the wider society and not just the chosen few. This was achieved by linking AI with blockchain technology, such that it would be secure from the bad actors.

The current banking system had accustomed people and industry to managing their money on line and the introduction of a new crypto currency was readily accepted and managed at minimal cost. Later hard currency could be minted and printed.

It is worth repeating that in generating funds for investment and a currency decoupled from Sterling (with the continued strengthening of society) we were now entering the point where more structured experienced and specialist leadership was needed; not the self-seeking politicians of Westminster but established altruistic local people with a known and established record of community support – a challenge that demanded the integration of wealth, leadership and society for the benefit of the County as a whole – the original driver originally behind establishing *The Thing* to develop a system where wealth (in particular societal[61] money) was managed locally and invested locally – whether into commerce, charity or not for profit organisations.

---

[61] Notes and coins in circulation; not the fiat money used by the 'investment bankers'.

This money was used to strengthen our various communities – caring, infrastructure, creativity and all the disparate things that go to make up a strong, vibrant and supportive society[62].

Preston – An Aside.

An excellent example of people taking back control is the town of Preston[63] which has successfully developed a programme of community wealth-building. The introduction notes.

At the heart of community wealth-building is the belief that ordinary individuals and groups are capable of taking ownership, direction and control of their own resources in order to improve their own lives. At a time when there is little prospect of economic transformation coming from Westminster, local action is an even more important source of hope and change.

Preston had delivered local self-sufficiency, The Thing had generated similar benefits but with a different mix of processes and across the County.

---

[62] To allow a degree of granularity (and regardless of the dictionary) society is made up of a number of (some times disparate) communities.

[63] *Paint your town red* ISBN 978-1-913462-19-2. Well worth a read.

Part 6. 2035 – What We Achieved.

Over the last decade we created an organisation that runs parallel to, and complementary with (yes, complementary with), the County-wide government run administration.

In getting to this point we identified historic let-downs by central government and events – both national and international – that would impact how the UK in general, and Yorkshire in particular, would be governed.

It was accepted that central government is too slow to change, and too much a beneficiary of the inequalities caused by unfair levels of investment determined by, for example, the Barnett formula. Action was needed on our part.

An alternative approach was instigated that united organisations, societies and people across the County, providing mutual support; later formalising that support into a time bank and subsequently a Yorkshire currency managed by our own Restoration Bank.

The bank was established as a retail bank, investing solely in local businesses with novel investment models and at a higher risk level than the established banks.

Innovation, inward investment and new markets were actively encouraged and supported such that the growth across Yorkshire supported increased investment which spilled over into reducing social inequality and improving services at all levels.

6.1 Looking Back From 2035.

<u>Core Purpose.</u>

The purpose had been to create an organisation that operated outside traditional government and was large enough and appropriately structured to be able to influence both national and local governments to the benefit of Yorkshire; redressing some of the inequalities that had grown up over the years, inequalities that had (apparently?) become locked into central government thinking.

A government thinking that seemed to have forgotten that its core functions were to:
- Protect the integrity of the realm and
- **Improve the lot of those within that realm.**

The organisation that emerged (The Thing) was established to evolve and adapt in an environment where internal and external forces were changing ever more rapidly. Some of the positive outcomes included:
- Created, and worked to, a clear objective,
- Ensured equality of support across the County,
- Delivered appropriate support and interventions,
- Encouraged local innovation and investment,
- Developed trading opportunities,
- Promoted alternative finance and investment, and
- Shared and signposted new technologies.

<u>Some Milestones.</u>

A clear objective was defined and articulated as noted above; this focused attention and the (normal?) tinkering at the edges could be left to others. This clear objective gave format to written documentation that informed actions and was clear to all; there was little room for personal interpretation of the more important issues. (included as appendix 3).

Given clarity of purpose for The Thing (not the individuals within it!) energy was focused to delivering on that purpose as was its administration. Superfluous measurements and 'nice to know' outputs were no longer generated, reducing unnecessary headcount, yet with the consequential increase in efficiency and productivity.

Given a clear objective and identifying the strands that went to delivering this objective, officers could be dedicated to particular tasks and outcomes, increasing the internal learning capacity whilst, as a consequence, reducing the risk profile for the organisation.

The most appropriate support could be directed to innovation and adding value (provided it met the organisation's core objective) and the best people drafted in to help deliver focused support optimally.

In having a clear objective, meetings could be called with real purpose (not 'because it's Monday morning') and with Stephen Covey goal of having the end in mind when starting.

Drawing together the various organisations, groups and people to a common purpose allowed The Thing to reach agreement on County-wide needs and logically determine priorities that could be agreed and achieved.

The priorities moved well beyond Westminster's various models and promises, focusing on social fairness, putting people before profit and supporting the arts, leisure and sports to improve wellbeing and lifestyle.

In having a County-wide perspective, support for commerce, value adding and innovation could be more equitably supported and investment directed to the most appropriate areas.

The support provided was more appropriate to the needs of an area or a particular demographic. For example, education[64] was focused on (local) future priorities and people having the capacity to improve themselves, their society, business or establishment.

Opportunities, generated in one area, could be directed for further development and support to another, perhaps more deprived, area.

---

[64] The purpose of education is surely to make people think, give them knowledge and understanding as a framework to support new thought, instil the curiosity that causes people to challenge and raise things to think about, and to then have the confidence to make suitable change for the better – whether academically or practically.

i.e. causes you to think, provides material to think with, supplies the enthusiasm to look for things to think about and the confidence to then apply that thinking.

Other elements such as transport were more closely aligned to peoples' needs, for example local agreements with cab firms replaced rural buses and served the more remote areas, helping people stay in touch or keep appointments.

Investment in infrastructure was managed according to need, not politicians' whims and fancies with the result that business could operate more efficiently and new organisations were attracted to the County which provided additional jobs and generated additional added value.

The dictum of managing and learning internally, occasionally making mistakes and sharing learning and knowledge led to fewer contractors, greater self-sufficiency and blame-free accountability which improved efficiency and reduced costs.

The establishment of The Thing included support from many walks of life and business, including a number of retirees with extensive experience and looking for something to do, those associated provided a cohort very able people to advise and support innovators and small businesses.

Such support included advisors using their contacts to set up mutual support opportunities (originally paid for by banked time), lead events and share skills that led to mutually beneficial introductions, also to deliver seminars on general matters and head groups to address specific problems. One-on-one support was provided where issues were specific or confidentiality a potential issue.

The breadth of experience of the advisors and their desire to continue to be involved in business provided a sounding-board for innovation and then the support to take the more likely successes forward for funding and more specialist support.

A good deal of advice was available for people with seriously viable ideas[65] including researching, planning, scheduling, financing and protecting the idea.

The established companies, in conjunction with the deep-water ports had a significant number of overseas contacts which included logistics, suppliers, customers and collaborators.

These personal contacts were shared to promote innovation, joint developments and investment in Yorkshire commerce and also the arts – music and theatre being established ways to bring people together.

In time, the alternative financial instruments, and developments with crypto, were used to create loans for inward investment creating jobs and interest from overseas companies keen to do business with Yorkshire and the UK.

This inward investment created new technologies for learning, teaching, dangerous jobs, public order and forecasting to note just a few applications.

---

[65] Please see Appendices 1 & 2 for notes about business planning and how a funder might read an application.

6.2 Looking Forward From 2035.

The fear with writing a book such as this is that it could reach an inadequate end (20 Yorkshire MPs trying to influence 300-odd party members) or is like a dog chasing a motorbike 'Now that I've caught it, what do I do with it?'

The long-term vision for Yorkshire and beyond is to take advantage of the slow changes to national governance, and create a situation for Yorkshire where:

- General elections are actually representative of the people voting.
- Money works for people – not the other way round.
- People across all socio-economic groups, societies and regions have dignity.
- Politics, commerce and society cooperate across borders, ideologies and cultures for the benefit of the County, not just the privileged few in London.
- A few elected Yorkshire MPs acting as a 'Ginger Group' exert a disproportionate impact on central government.

Could Yorkshire enjoy the same amount of direct influence when a divided Westminster has a weak party in charge?

Since 2024, the people of Yorkshire have worked to build a society where communities are supported, governments have been forced to listen, there is a more equitable distribution of investment, we have high levels of employment, an innovative culture and people want to invest. How did we get here?

A Reprise.

As the local generation of wealth begins to bite and the management of that wealth becomes important there are various considerations and interconnections that are quite complex and perhaps best introduced as an analogy with a cruise liner.

The cruise liner has a bridge where the captain directs, an engine room that provides the motive energy and a crew who have joined for a fulfilling life as a mariner.

These three parties have to work harmoniously together, and with purpose – to give the passengers a fulfilling experience time so that they will return.

Let us now replace the engine room with wealth – the energy to move forward; replace the crew with society – structured to fulfil the needs and wishes of the people; and replace the bridge with leadership – selected to give purpose and direction to the integrated whole.

The structure was established and driven forward in much the same way as the explorers and settlers took over America, Australia and other nation states.

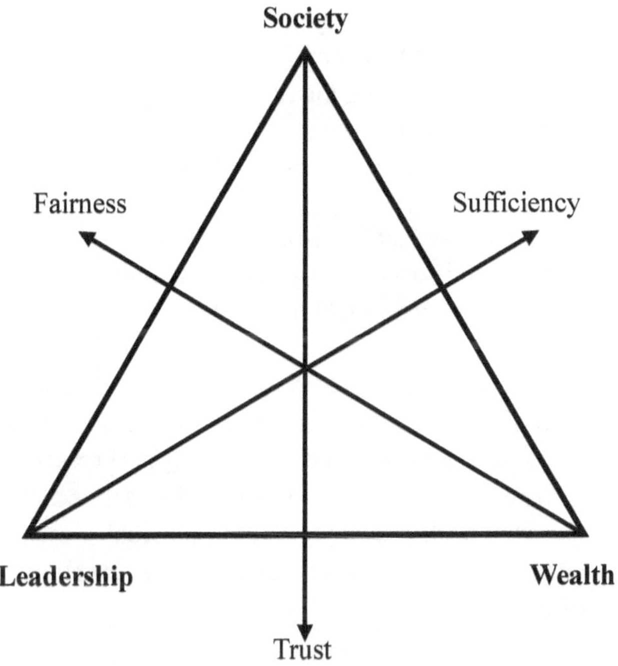

The various roles are inter-related in that:

- Wealth will be directed fairly to ensure sustainability and be invested where best used to benefit society.
- Society will trust the leadership to manage the wealth purposefully and for enriching the lives of all, not just a select few.
- Leadership will ensure sufficiency of wealth to allow society to grow and flourish for the particular needs and overall benefit of the various communities.

Since 2027 organisations worked cooperatively for mutual benefit where the rewards were enjoyed by all concerned and continually developed:
- Wealth promoting dignity in Society.
- Society giving Leadership purpose.
- Leadership ensuring sustainability of Wealth.

A virtuous and dynamic cycle linking dignity, purpose and sustainability, all combining to deliver a more respected Yorkshire into the future.

The model was picked up by other communities with similar dynamics and where citizenship is as much an attitude of mind as it is a physical presence.

The first society to follow a similar path was the Geordies with a distinct culture, regional presence and significant dissatisfaction with being the puppets of party politics.

<u>Appendices.</u>

App. 1. A Fresh Look At Money.

Whatever system of governance, society or commerce is developed it will always be underpinned by a financial arrangement that enables exchange of goods and services; yet, such a practice is little more than a belief system[66] and, just like a belief, can take many forms.

Below, is an examination of money starting with a consideration that the system has been one of people working for the sake of money when, surely, money should be working for the sake of people (Copernicus).

During the early years of the 21st century a number of alternative currencies emerged alongside those established over centuries; however, some depended on technology and technology kept evolving such that a number of these currencies saw their demise and subsequent resurrection; (see below Countdown to Recession, Appendix 1.2).

Part of the loss in the value of money was the deregulation of the banks and them pushing the envelope in all directions on order to try to create yet more money – which is, after all, an imaginary concept (Fractional Reserve Banking).

Finally, a consideration of how economics might be reconsidered to add to the traditional belief in money and offer various options might be developed to complement, and perhaps influence, traditional economic thinking (A Fresh Look At Economics)

---

[66] Please see Philip Goodchild *Theology of Money*

1.1. Copernicus.

Some time ago I wrote a paper entitled *Copernicus, where are you now?* In which the discovery that the earth rotates around the sun was ignored by those in power and only became public after they retired or died.

The second half of the paper is a repeat, using the same words as far as possible to consider money being the focus and people rotating around it, when in reality it's money that should be revolving around people.

I've reproduced the paper here, followed by some thoughts about alternative ways of looking at economics.

Copernicus.

As far as possible the same words have been used to describe how astronomy took a step-change and why a parallel step-change is now appropriate for the financial world to move from the few with the most to begin (at last) to make finance work for the good of the many.

It may be argued that this would demand a new economical model which moves on from the model of continued growth (which surely has to stop somewhere?)

Masters of the Universe.

The universe started from a cloud of swirling dust and gas which coalesced into centres that progressively grew and grew to develop into planets, suns and other celestial bodies that we know today.

For about a thousand years people believed the Earth to be the centre of the universe and the heavens rotated around it, as described by Aristotle and Ptolemy who created a 'layers of the onion' model with the Moon, Mercury, Venus, Sun, Mars, Jupiter, Saturn and finally the fixed stars in nested shells with the earth at the centre.

When observations, measurement and recording were quite primitive this worked well and described the universe in understandable ways and gave some substance to astrology where the constellations move from 'house' to 'house' in the outer layer of the onion and so influence everything contained within this outer shell.

As observation, measurement and reporting improved, strange phenomena began to be noted such as the movement of Mars that follows a strange heart-shaped path across the sky known as a limaçon, where its orbit appears to loop back on itself for a short period.

Ways to explain this had to be found if the model was to remain credible.

As astronomical observation improved further additional layers had to be added to explain the increasing complexity:

- The Platonic system moved the sun inside the orbits of mercury and Venus,
- The Egyptian system put Mercury and Venus revolving around the Sun with the Sun and other planets revolving around the Earth,

- The Tychonic system described the Sun and Moon revolving around the Earth and all the other planets revolving around the Sun,
- The last of the major earth-centred models was that of Giovanni Riccioli where Mercury, Mars and Venus orbit the Sun and the Sun, Jupiter and Saturn orbit the Earth.

This is a wonderful example of complexity developed by brilliant minds to define and describe a model that was flawed – a model that lasted for over a thousand years, supported by those with vested interests such as the various religions that put humanity at the centre of everything.

In a similar way, for many years we have put finance at the centre of everything, supported by those with vested interests such as the landowners, oligarchs and the major accountancy firms that support these vested interests.

Thankfully, in the sixteenth century, Copernicus arrived and put the Sun at the Centre of the known universe and created a much simpler model that predicted the positions of the planets, stars and natural phenomena such as eclipses (which had caused so much anxiety in earlier times).

Developments continued, and continue to better understand the nature of the universe and all within it.

Interestingly, the Copernican model remained in the background for about fifty years before people took serious notice - about the time it would take those with personal vested interest to either retire or pass on.

The story continues to evolve as newer and better descriptions are developed to describe the ever increasing understanding and complexity of the universe. However, the description of our unfolding knowledge so far is adequate to draw parallels with the financial systems we have today.

The Egyptian view of the solar system.

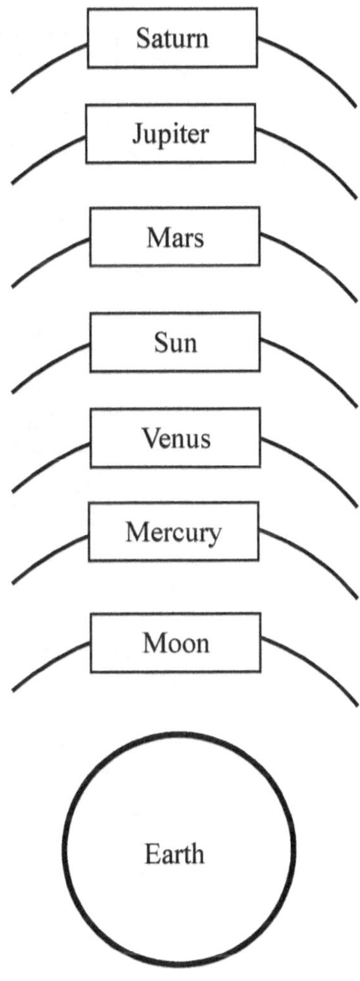

The Copernican view of the solar system.

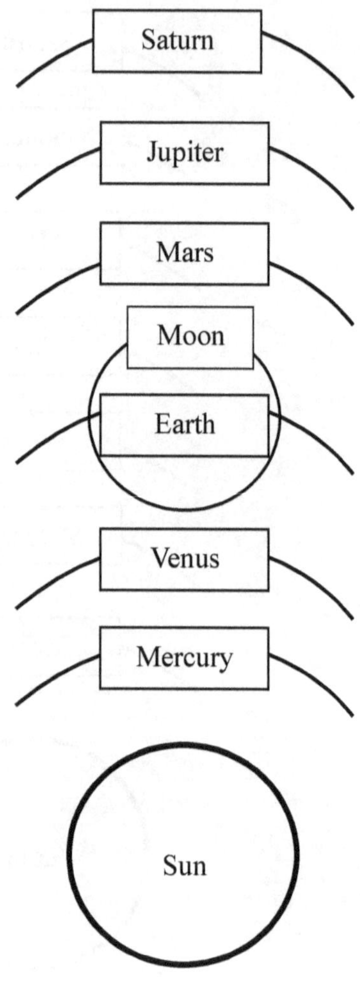

Saturn
Jupiter
Mars
Moon
Earth
Venus
Mercury
Sun

Financial Parallels.

In the beginning, people traded wool, eggs or their skills in order to improve their quality of life but ran into trouble converting a dozen eggs into a quantity of wool, or a haircut. So, in time, these different values and trading standards coalesced into precious metals and got called 'money'.

In the early days in the UK a pound (£) was just that – a pound (lb) of pure silver which could be divided and exchanged for goods and services.

However, silver is quite bulky and as medieval inflation took hold the gold standard was introduced, using a more valuable metal to keep the weight down and in time, promissory notes were invented to take the place of bulky metal.

Today, no-one ever uses a physical pound with which to trade; just the belief that the pound represented by the paper is worth what's printed on it. Money is imaginary!

This 'money' took on a belief all of its own and the theology of money (see Philip Goodchild) led to it becoming the centre of the universe – like the Earth of ancient times; and where all human life and activity revolves around it – wellbeing, poverty, ownership, power and all the other trappings that define today's 'civilised society'.

Accompanying this argenticentric universe went a number of observations and rudimentary calculations where the original theories were represented by the normal distribution (see Mandelbrot *The (Mis)behaviour of Markets*.

This worked well until new instruments were discovered – a bit like the observation of additional planets and moons in medieval times – and so various correction factors, betas and various constants were added [by people who should know better] to explain the deviant behaviours of a system that has finance at its centre and people somewhere in the planetary Kuyper belt.

As with cosmology, various stellar clouds (Dollars, Pounds, Euros and all the other currencies) have coalesced into the celestial bodies we call Switzerland, British Virgin Islands, Belize and other centres of gravity, which sit at the centre of things.

Recently, with increasing transparency, crude observations are being made of the financial universe by outsiders who are now challenging the 'layers of the onion' model with the investment and merchant bankers at the centre of the universe and omnipotent, taking risk with other peoples' money to deliver what they think should be theirs; whilst everything else revolves around them.

The second layer of this onion is the retail bankers, taking less risk with other peoples' money but acting as a feed to the merchant bankers and investment bankers and successive layers include:

- Commerce, which provides the activities that generate the (imaginary?) money through trade whilst providing a vehicle for the investment bankers to rake risks with.

- The workforce, which acts within commerce to provide the labour and energy to drive the commercial engine.
- Traders who act as intermediaries between the creators of goods and services and the users.
- Buyers who make use of the goods and services to improve their lifestyle.
- Society, which forms the outer layer, like stars in the night sky and generally predictable.

In addition, there are individuals with a great deal of personal wealth orbiting the centre of the universe like planets in their own right, whether wealthy politicians, successful entrepreneurs or determined criminals – each describing their own limaçon or having their orbit around another 'heavenly body' – like a moon.

<u>So where is Copernicus now we need him?</u>

By taking a direct parallel to the development of cosmological understanding in the middle ages we have a system that may be represented by the diagrams below.

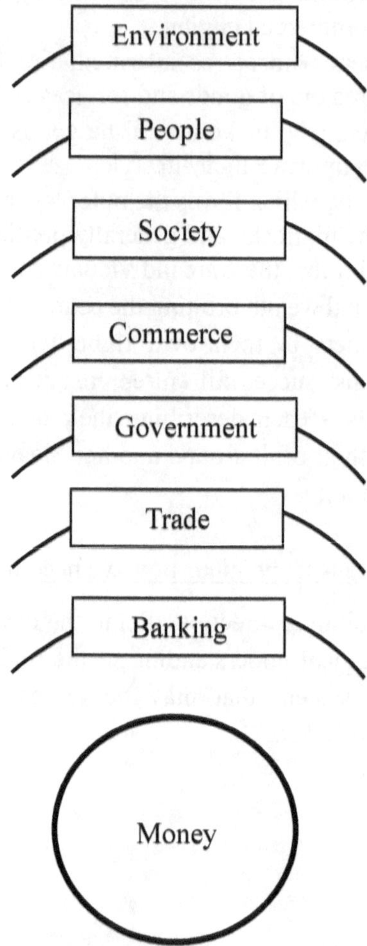

People and the environment very much removed from money (and the creation of money).

But surely people should be at the centre with the financial activities serving their needs.

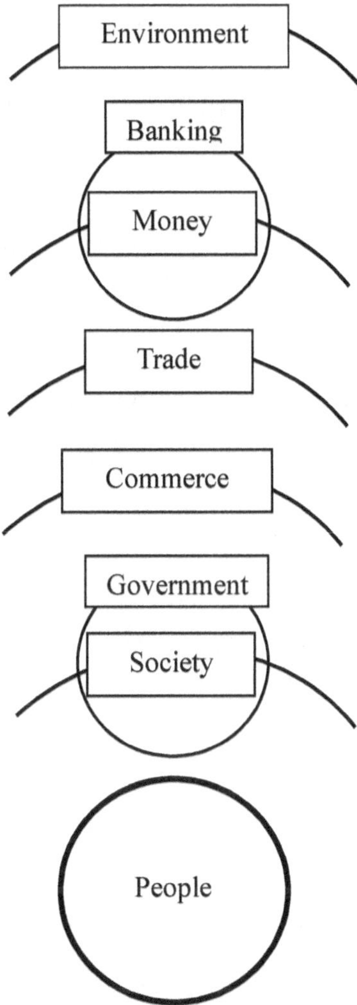

People now at the centre with money revolving around them; but, the environment, sadly (and frighteningly) will most likely remain peripheral.

In Conclusion.

Money has now become the servant and is no longer the master – we have removed the need for a belief system and can trade in actualities rather than promises.

And, on a sobering note, after many discussions it appears that the one element which will continue to sit outside this model is the environment – and in the longer-term we may all drown in a sludge of our commercial making – however we might decide to position money and people.

1.2. Countdown To Recession[67].

<u>2024. Cryptocoin Recovery Landmark Cases.</u>

People defrauded of crypto currencies have been unable to recover their losses from the 'banks' which have claimed their distributed nature absolves them of a central responsibility; yet, changes cannot be made without the express approval of a few key players. The crypto narrative was broken.

- Digital Asset Recovery (https://bit.ly/3KizSgP).
- Second order effects cause delay in halls of wealth & power.
- West exits Ukraine, lowering prices, boosting productivity.

<u>2025. Cryptocoin Collapse.</u>

The 'arms-length', 'hands-off' stance by those who manage the cryptosphere has disguised significant fraud internally as well as external fraud and money laundering.

- Crypto exchanges fraud and crypto CEOs fraud lead to high profile jailings.
- General confidence lost in cryptocurrencies; blockchains head to zero.
- Bankers & politicians discovered to be deeply involved in crypto – the real culprits.

---

[67] Several versions were circulating; would like to acknowledge the originator, but not sure who that is.

2026 – First Half. Mortgage Trigger.

The investment of fiat money and also crypto into dodgy mortgage dossiers (again) sees property prices rise as investors try to hang onto their apparent wealth by finding another round of greedy opportunists.

- Mortgage repossessions climb, transactions fall and property prices peak.
- Fake news can't hold out, the start of authentic reports into what's happening.
- Crypto fraud spills over into the regular financial markets.

2026 – Second Half. The Great Recession.

The banks which had been professing to avoid crypto because of its volatility and lack of accountability have actually been investing in it and the Bank of England has been using crypto for at least eight years for immediate settlements. The government, adopting a hands-off stance in case they get things wrong and risk losing votes stand by until it's too late for decisive action.

- The level of banks' exposure to worthless crypto stakes and levels of fraud is exposed.
- Global financial markets shown to be mainly mortgage derivatives. Assets fall 40% in days.
- Confidence lost as banks become insolvent.
- Government late to act, blame greed, CEOs & the wealthy but hide homeowner speculation.

<u>2027 – 2031. The Great Recovery.</u>

The government stops sitting on its hands and decides something needs to be done. The change of government from Conservative means the elite and privileged are not as well protected as when the bubble burst. Socialist governments focus on the people, not the wealthy elite.

- House prices bottom, ecash and financial alternatives assist significantly.
- Governments bail out defaulting homeowners.
- Banks rejuvenated, a new cycle begins[68].

---

[68] Please see https://bit.ly/3QjZSfw

1.3. Fractional Banking.

In order to tell the story, all figures have been kept to round numbers and easy sums; substituting current figures does not change the story, simply refines it a bit.

<u>The story we're expected to believe.</u>

As a starting hypothesis, imagine I go into the bank and deposit £1,000. The bank pays me 5% p.a. interest and lends the money deposited at 10% p.a. interest.

I get paid £50 and the bank makes £100 – a net margin to the bank of 5% on the year. Years ago, I was told by the Midland Bank (as was) that their average net margin after paying overheads was 2.4%; i.e. only one loan in 40 had to turn sour for the bank to make a loss, and I believed them (but see below).

The 5%, used here as an example, is compared by the bankers to a commercial company which makes around a 28% net margin but has to pay for amortisation, depreciation, leases and things normally quite low on banks' scale of priorities; nevertheless major commercial organisations (FTSE 350) in 1998/1999 made around 8.5% profit[69], which is roughly three times that professed by the banks and what we are supposed to believe.

---

[69] Please see *Does Business Ethics Pay* ISBN 0 9539517 3 1 Appendix 4.

When is a liability not a liability? – When it's a Reserve.

When you make a deposit with a bank that money should be, technically, a liability in their balance sheet because you can claim it back at any time and it is not, technically, the bank's property[70].

However, through what appears to have been a bit of historical collusion between the political and banking elites, your deposit, in law!, now becomes the property of the bank and can be reclassified as a ***Reserve*** – a simple change of words (politicians are good at this) which, by sleight of hand, gets rid of all that messy business which goes with double-entry bookkeeping.

Now that the bank's Liability has become a Reserve, it can be treated as if it was an Asset and loaned to people wanting to borrow.

However several centuries ago, it was recognised that not everyone would seek to withdraw their deposited money from the bank all at once and

---

[70] This is paralleled by the major supermarkets who 'invite' suppliers to make a 'pre-payment' which is little more than a bribe, paid quarterly <u>in advance</u>, to secure a bit of extra shelf space; in strict accounting terms this is technically a liability because, in theory, the supplier could claim it back.

Tesco got caught out in 2014 when they reported prepayments as an asset to notionally boost their returns from trading by about £600m. The company refused to say whether this was intentional or through incompetence – but either way there were resignations!

therefore it was not necessary to keep all the money deposited available for withdrawal.

Banks then realised that they could lend beyond their means and no-one would notice.

Money could be conjured out of thin air and the banks could (modestly) lend beyond their asset base to increase profitability beyond the 2.4% professed (see above, and remember Northern Rock).

To prevent this creation of money getting out of hand it would appear that the bankers and the politicians got together again to limit the amount of imaginary (fiat – let there be) money that could be conjured by creating an instrument called the Fractional Reserve.

The Fractional Reserve.

At the time of writing, the Fractional Reserve for Banks is 12½% i.e. they can create out of nowhere seven times the money actually held on deposit; and for Finance Houses (including Investment Banks) this fraction is 10%. i.e. nine times deposited money (whether real or imaginary).

Sticking with the banks, this means that they can advance seven times their (declared) assets as interest bearing loans and, assuming the Bank of England is doing its job, and all this fiat money can be turned into loans. The bank (charging 10% remember) can turn an actual £1,000 into a fiat £7,000 and create an additional £700 in interest. i.e.

The fractional reserve has allowed the bank to recoup interest on:

£1,000 original deposit (real money) £100

£7,000 fractional reserve (fiat money) £700

And pay the depositor £(50) for the privilege of using their (now the bank's) money.

A net return of £750, or 75% against the 5% they would have us believe.

Occasionally, a bank might overstretch and go beyond the agreed fraction which led to the creation of the 'Clearing Banks' – which includes most of the High Street Banks we know today. What happens is that the banks 'clear down' their assets and liabilities at the end of trading to the Bank of England.

The Bank of England (outside of direct government control) 'lends' funds from one bank that has underused its fractional reserve to a bank that has been a bit enthusiastic, thereby ensuring each bank sits within the legal terms of its fractional reserve.

The next day, the banks clear down again and debts repaid; new debts emerge, matched by new 'loans' and the system gets rebalanced to ensure the banking system as a whole can maximise its profits within the strictures of the law.

The interesting irony in all this is that the extra £7,000 loaned is imaginary money – it wasn't generated by any means other than as an entry in a spreadsheet. Nothing was created, no value-added, no skills or experience necessary.

And as for the repayments – these are made in real money earned by someone adding value, providing skills and delivering tangible benefit.

So here we are, the banks lend imaginary money in order to suck real money out of the economy to pay the bankers significant bonuses and their shareholders impressive returns.

A fraud of global proportions, and where else would you see share value increase as liabilities increase? Please see *High Finance* below.

<u>Investment Banking.</u>

And the fraud doesn't end there; with deregulation of the banks by Thatcher & Regan (followed by other finance centres soon after) the banks elaborated their own Finance Houses to take surplus uninvested depositors' fractionally reserved money (still balanced by the Bank of England) to invest in enterprises of all shapes and sizes.

Of note is that the Investment Banks' credit ratings are the highest possible with the Clearing Banks, simply because they are part of the same organisation – and as such, have little difficulty in arranging a loan and that these loans can be amplified (remember the finance houses' fractional reserve is only 10%) and turned into yet more imaginary money for investment into dodgy tech, bubbles and insider rumours.

This imaginary money generates dividends for the investors and is paid in real money generated by organisations adding value, providing skills and delivering benefit.

<u>Fraud upon fraud upon fraud.</u>

- Fraud 1.   Converting depositors' money into a Reserve which can be treated as if an asset.
- Fraud 2.   Creating loans from nothing and charging real money as interest.
- Fraud 3.   Investing imaginary money in rumour and insider dealing to pay dividends in real money.

<u>The escalated value of your deposit.</u>

Your deposit   £1,000
Bank's £1,000 Fractional Reserve now   £7,000
Investment Bank's £7,000 Fractional Reserve now becomes £63,000 (10% Fraction creates 9x the original sum); and, as if by magic, the banks has now escalated the 'value' of your deposit 62 times. This seems reasonably consistent with approximately £100bn in circulation and £13tn total UK wealth (which probably also includes foreign investment).

<u>And it doesn't end there.</u>

The removal of circulating (real) money from the economy is bad enough because there is less opportunity for people to purchase things which results in commerce (keen to pay dividends) raising prices to increase margins which reduces further the money people have to support their lifestyles.

So, the government now asks the Bank of England to issue additional imaginary money (as government bonds) supported by the Clearing Banks

Reserves and Reserve Fractions – no doubt based on another fractional reserve calculation.

These bonds are interest bearing which sucks more real money from the economy through taxation and (wait for it) ***austerity***. This is euphemistically called *Quantitative Easing* – I wonder who dreamed up that term for a governmental Ponzi scheme?

To cover the cost of this historic profligacy we now enter another period of austerity – a time span with no discernible end point and which involves the raising of interest rates to reduce spending – which can be a bit tricky if you have nothing to spend!

<u>Yet more dodgy dealing.</u>

Normally tax is paid on earnings and we are led to believe it will be re-invested in supporting and developing UK societies and people that are disadvantaged – a process of 'levelling up'.

However, taxes can be avoided (not evaded, there's a distinction) through clever manipulation of tax loopholes and mechanisms that don't get closed because they are needed by governments to manage an even higher level of fraud[71]. The scope and complexity of which is outside this short note but there is plenty of information on-line.

Big enough companies establish their head offices in 'tax-efficient' locations including Ireland, Luxembourg and the Caymen Islands which avoids paying UK Corporation Tax.

---

[71] Please see *Capitalism's Achilles Heel* by Raymond Baker ISBN 0-471-64488-9.

Wealthy individuals may avoid paying income tax by being defined as non-domiciled and having addresses registered in the places noted above or even behind a brass plate in some distant land.

All of which denies tax from profit & income generated in the UK to invest back into UK society.

<u>And there's more.</u>

Progressive governments have encouraged overseas organisations to 'invest' in the UK by offering incentives to build factories and provide jobs. Incentives that make politicians look good by delivering high employment figures (fewer job-seekers, what a euphemism!) but with any net profit and dividends from these organisations being repatriated to the countries whose companies have 'invested' in the UK – China, France and the Middle East to name but three.

So we collect income tax but miss out on corporation tax. At the time of writing we have also missed out on foreign companies investing in programmed maintenance and infrastructure replacement in their scramble to maximise shareholder returns. A lack of investment which the UK government may well pick up and remedy through renationalisation (and at UK taxpayers' expense).

And, remember, it doesn't matter if the water doesn't flow; trains don't run and roads seize up – their owners are somewhere overseas and it doesn't impact on their lifestyles; so, why should they care?

<u>Inflation.</u>

Inflation is an increase in the quantity of money with a balancing decrease in its value (my definition). And where does inflation come from? Can I suggest:

* Clearing banks fractional reserve of 12½ %,
* Investment banks fractional reserve of 10 %,
* Tax avoidance by the wealthy,
* Tax avoidance by organisations,
* Repatriation of profits and a need to now invest in dilapidated infrastructure.

All supported by *quantitative easing* and paid for by the have-nots through austerity, society through crumbling infrastructure and commerce through reduced investment.

<u>In summary.</u>

The UK has a history of bankers' (legalised) fraud, support for the already wealthy (whether organisations. politicians or individuals) and chronic political neglect of the country's value-adding facilities and infrastructure; focusing instead on banking, investment and the City of London.

The cost of resurrecting a meaningful lifestyle for millions of people will be immense and those millions of people are suffering increasing austerity whilst banks stand back and government feigns ignorance and powerlessness – advised by economists who pretend it's the peoples' fault.

Good here – Innit?

1.4. A Fresh Look At Economics.

<u>Lies, Damn Lies and …</u>

Statistics; a bit technical.

Interestingly, members of the Office for National Statistics (ONS) appeared increasingly uncomfortable talking about average wages when interviewed by media people; this was quite understandable when the statistical average is based on a normal distribution (bell-shaped curve) but as the distribution of pay levels became increasingly skewed the ONS stuck with the average because it made the tax cuts for the wealthy appear more equitable.

Surely a calculation such as the median would give a more honest view. However, as the politicians stuck to the misleading view, the statisticians got increasingly uneasy.

Not only were averages reported inaccurately, investment was distributed unequally, based on the 'Barnett formula' – a formula that Joel Barnett himself said was flawed; it's based on how much the block funding should change each year based on the previous year – so if, year one provided inadequate funding, this inadequacy will be multiplied in subsequent years. There is no allowance for emerging need, remediation or for any corrective activity.

This applies to devolved governments and also to departments, so *Levelling-up* would be linked to this formula.

The formula isn't enshrined in law, it is a policy that the Treasury chooses to follow. It was introduced as a temporary measure in the late 1970s but, with no commitment to replace it, the Barnett formula looks like being around to celebrate its 40th anniversary in the not too distant future[72].

By 2035, things had changed to more accurately compute the figures, taking into account social needs as well as bankers and shareholders demands for ever increasing returns.

Some of the balance was made up by alternative currencies and time banks as discussed above, leading to a fairer and more equitable distribution of wealth.

It's About More Than Money.

Whatever happens we need money in order to change things for the better; this will involve a sympathetic fiscal policy. Monetary policy will look after itself, being dependent solely on how much money finds its way into our banking system (See below The Local Growth Fund which was originally established in Burnley as The Bank of Dave).

Managing the fiscal policy will be a new kind of politician – of the people, remember – not some self-centred mendacious wobblegob of the kind that has contaminated Westminster for decades.

---

[72] https://commonslibrary.parliament.uk/the-barnett-formula-a-quick-guide/ 2023

<u>Better Taxation.</u>

With more equitable taxation we could all benefit – the poor at the expense of the very rich (Robbin' Hood) please see Prof. Richard Murphy, Sheffield University Management School's reports prepared on behalf of Finance for the Future LLP[73].

The full report came out towards the end of 2023 but even now, in 2035, public sector intransigence, and sitting politicians' 'sponsors' interests meant that not enough had been done. The Thing is now influential enough to cause a number of Prof. Murphy's recommendations to start to be implemented; these were:
- Taxing the wealthiest people.
- Taxing the high earners.

Despite overlap, both groups were considerably under-taxed by the UK legacy tax system. Additional reforms to types of tax and administrative overheads could raise up to £100bn P.A. The more significant reforms were:
- Abolishing VAT exemption on financial services £8bn.
- Reforming NI charges on high earners raised £12bn.
- Aligning capital gains and income tax raised £12bn.
- Increasing corporation for the largest companies £7bn.

---

[73] https://taxingwealth.uk/
https://www.taxresearch.org.uk/Blog/about/

- Reforming the administration of corporation tax £6bn.
- Reforming Companies House raised about £6bn.

The legacy of excessive administrative overheads goes back several decades and the sums here could, no doubt, be increased. A paper from the early 2000s lays out a similar argument[74].

None of this 'undertaxation' is new and there was little to encourage the right level across big business, banking and the already wealthy.

The Wrong Money.

The money taken in taxation has traditionally been societal money, not the bankers' fiat money that has led (and continues to lead) to so much misery for many.

For example, suppose a bank has built up expertise in a given commercial sector and, as a result, through lending to investors is heavily exposed in that sector, it only needs one of the larger organisations to have a couple of bad quarters when spoilers on social media can spread despondency and panic.

Shares are unloaded increasingly rapidly to reduce 'exposure' and then shares in other, similar, organisations are unloaded and the bank can't afford the losses.

---

[74] https://fundamentally.typepad.com/files/lets-get-real-with-the-national-debt.pdf

So we see a familiar pattern emerging – governments bail out the bank and all is sweet. Except, previous profits have been privatised, current losses are socialised and not a single investment banker sees the bailiff turn up to repossess a mansion, a yacht or a Rolls Royce.

We needed something different and reliable; an alternative approach needed to be developed which is how the Local Growth Funds came about.

<u>Society And Alternative Finance.</u>

As noted above, people began to take matters into their own hands, and move away from money as we know it; starting with time-banks which worked well provided the location was discrete and tightly-knit; and, that someone had the time to manage the various transactions.

Unfortunately time credits and debits could not be readily traded outside the particular community but, through the intervention of The Thing, adjacent communities began to work together and 'trade' across the boundaries – still within a very narrow compass.

At the same time, Bartercard was trying to make a comeback but not very successfully and someone had the bright idea to turn time into a currency – after all, what is a currency but a belief system; this was actually more tangible than existing currencies created at a stroke on a spreadsheet[75].

---

[75] See section above about banking; also, *The Theology of Money* by Phillip Goodchild.

A new currency was born mirroring *Ithaca Hours*. With Ithaca Hours the currency of measured time is represented in a printed format; but, by 2026 technology had reached a point where a time-based currency could be managed as a block-chain[76] and integrated between social clusters.

In due course, this time-based currency became

The Yorkshire Rose (℞) and was managed by The Restoration Bank which dealt simply as a retail bank without any investment activity and with a lower fractional reserve than traditional banking (see below). It did, however, charge interest which was used to support local investment.

The pieces of the jigsaw were coming together to provide alternative support for local innovation.

The Thing banked with The Restoration Bank which managed both Sterling and crypto currency, based on the net value of Yorkshire (underpinning the Yorkshire Rose) which has a value that changes depending on added value per working person, and also traditional Sterling.

Deposits were generated from the banking of subscriptions, philanthropic donors, grants, and time. Loans were advanced from these deposits and interest charged – but not necessarily as a percentage of a (reducing?) principal.

---

[76] Blockchain technology, properly configured and well managed is immune to hacking; even with AI based systems.

<u>More Financial Freedom.</u>

The new banking approach was based on the principle that (where possible) funds should be invested where they are generated.

This investment dictum was used by The Thing to pay (at least) the expenses of the various advisors supporting business development & innovation and, importantly, for investments beyond the immediate purchase of assets, advertising or wages to people newly hired to develop the business.

The format of the investment was not necessarily financial, it could be in the form of hours accumulated in the various time banks.

Finance was, however the most common form of investment and could be as a traditional loan bearing interest and repayable as interest plus a proportion of the (diminishing) capital at regular intervals.

An alternative approach was to give a value to the organisation three years out and provide a loan as a fixed[77] proportion of the projected equity, ensure funds were set aside each year, take dividends and in three years recalculate the equity and redeem the loan.

---

[77] Making the load as a <u>fixed</u> proportion of the equity avoided the investment banks' trick of making up any shortfall in payment be additional equity after providing an 'advisor' who runs the business down until the bank 'owns' 75% of the organisation. At which point the 'advisor' becomes quite astute, grows the organisation; the bank sells it in a pre-arranged sale and makes an additional killing. All very honourable!

The downside of this form of investment in the business might be that growth is held back due to dividends and money being set aside for future repayment; the upside is that the organisation can get off to a good start with three years to become established.

Each system has merits and potential problems, and each will suit one venture more than another.

A further development to investment is a willingness to fund the expansion of an innovation, too often a business develops a prototype and banks refuse to fund development because it might be a bit risky.

The risk assessments were revised in favour of the innovator to keep new ideas and opportunities within the County and not taken 'abroad' for development with profits being repatriated overseas.

A Summary of Alternative Economics.

Government statistics are deliberately misleading for example the use of 'average' for pay and taxation, the word 'average is pretty much meaningless in statistical terms where *Collins Dictionary of Statistics* notes that "According to context [average], may be any (or none) of mean, mode, median or midrange."

The distribution of wages and taxes is anything but a normal distribution, being heavily skewed to those with and hiding the real position of those without.

Since about 1995 there has been a trend to maximise returns – a move away from delivering benefits to society. Whilst a few have got rich, the many have been ignored.

There has been a growing need to fairer taxation in order to generate the funds to better develop society; additionally, a review of taxation to pick off the various derogations and loopholes could provide a significant boost to the Westminster Treasury (but at a cost to the rich and connected).

The growth in money has been through 'fiat' money – imaginary stuff created out of thin air on the back of fractional reserve banking.

Such money risks destabilising the banks and the entire financial system – 2028 saw just such an eventuality; alternative forms of finance were needed to provide some security and safety to the local monetary situation.

This balance of risk allowed the County to innovate, grow and begin to invest back into society – thereby beginning to regain our humanity and reduce our dependence (as a puppet) on Westminster and its associated inequalities.

1.5. Caution With The New Economy.

The possibility of an alternative economy, designed to keep funds and investments circulating within the County and not subject to manipulation by Westminster is very attractive and a bigger project than attempted elsewhere, but a big project is not an issue if managed well i.e.

- Multiple local time banks established.
- Local time-bank hours developed into a bankable and transferrable form of credit (see Ithaca).
- A 'Bank of Dave' clone, called The Restoration Bank was established to coordinate the various time banks across the County.
- The Restoration Bank also dealt in sterling which was deposited as Membership fees, loans, grants and philanthropic donations.
- The transferrable hours were turned into a local currency – The Yorkshire Rose.
- The Yorkshire Rose was developed into a tradeable County-wide currency.
- A blockchain variation of the Yorkshire Rose was created to more readily facilitate local trade.
- The logic of the 1932 Rentenmark, Yuan & Ruble was used to develop cross-border trade.
- The value of the Yorkshire Rose was linked to the EVA per working person within the County which avoided inflation.
- The Restoration Bank collected interest, made loans to invest in Yorkshire business and innovation.
- Value created was kept within the County for the benefit of the County.

The key issue in this exercise was managing the rate of roll-out because loans granted immediately take a number of years to realise their full repayment and interest.

An example of how this time difference can escalate and cause significant embarrassment is described well by Peter Senge's *Beer Game*[78].

The principles of this discussion can be adapted to other settings e.g. NHS waiting lists and was used as a format to manage the controlled roll-out of funds and banking services across Yorkshire.

The more complete story is the subject of a separate study to explore economics in greater depth and with relevance to a more contemporary setting[79] which does not assume equilibriums, or that the entirety of society behaves like one happy family[80].

---

[78] Peter Senge, The Fifth Discipline, ISBN 0-7126-5687-1 published in 1990. Pp. 27ff.

[79] As taught at Leeds University

[80] Steve Keen, The New Economics, ISBN 978-1509-545-292 Pg.132.

App. 2 The Rules Of The Garage.

These rules were put down by Bill Hewlett and David Packard when they originated their business that became international and very influential. They still hold good for a fledgeling enterprise as well as for an established one.

- Believe you can change the world.
- Work quickly, keep the tools unlocked, work whenever.
- Know when to work alone and when to work together.
- Share — tools, ideas. Trust your colleagues.
- No Politics. No bureaucracy. (These are ridiculous in a garage.)
- The customer defines a job well done.
- Radical ideas are not bad ideas.
- Invent different ways of working.
- Make a contribution every day. If it doesn't contribute, it doesn't leave the garage.
- Believe that together we can do anything.
- Invent.

App. 3. A Written Constitution.

The written constitution and framework for governance contained the themes noted below:

1   Name of Organisation.

2.   Purpose of the Constitution.

3   Vision and Objectives.
3.1 Vision.
3.2 Objective.

4   Values and Principles.
4.1 Statement of values.
4.2 Further values & Principles.

5   Membership.

6   Equal Opportunities.

7   Public Office.

8   Organisation.

9   Management.
9.1 Committees.
9.2 Officers:
Leader
Treasurer
Nominating Officer
Chair

Posted on the website.

Bibliography

<u>Economics.</u>

Banerjee et al A. 2019, Good Economics For Hard Times, Allan Lane, ISBN 978-0-241-30689-5

Barker. R, 2001, Determining Value, Pearson Education, ISBN 0-273-63979-X

Booth. J, 2020, The Price Of Tomorrow, Stanley, ISBN 978-1-999-25740-8

Earle et. al. J, 2017, The Econocracy, Penguin, ISBN 978-0-141-98696-9

Feierstein. M. 2012, Planet Ponzi, Black Swan, ISBN 978-0-552-77827-5

Harford. T. 2006, The Undercover Economist, Abacus, ISBN, 978-0-349-11985-4

Keen. S. 2022, The New Economics, Polity, ISBN 978-1-509-54529-2

Keen. S. 2017, Can We Avoid Another Financial Crisis? Polity, ISBN 978-1-509-51373-4

Kolle. et al. T. 2011, Value, Wiley, ISBN 978-0-470-42460-5

Mandelbrot. B. 2004, The (Mis)Behaviour Of Markets, Perseus, ISBN 978-1-846-68262-9

Milanovic. B. 2016, Global Inequality, Harvard, ISBN 978-0-674-98403-5

Smith. A. 1784, The Wealth Of Nations 2000 edition, Random House, ISBN 0-679-78336-9

Thaler. R. 2015, Misbehaving, Penguin, ISBN 978-0-241-95122-4

Thomas. E. 2020, 99%, Apollo, ISBN 978-1-789-54451-0

<u>Politics.</u>

Bullough. O. 2022, Butler To The World, Profile, ISBN 978-1-788-16587-7

Curry. J. 2023, Climate Uncertainty And Risk, ISBN 978-1-839-98925-4

Duncan. A. 2021, In The Thick Of It, William Collins, ISBN 978-0-008-42226-4

Esler. G. 2021, How Britain Ends. Apollo, ISBN 978-1-800-24105-3

Jones. O. 2014, The Establishment, Penguin, ISBN 978-0-141-97499-6

Jones. D. 2011, Fixing Britain, Wiley, ISBN 978-0-470-97763-7

Letts. Q. 2017, Patronising Bastards, Constable, ISBN 978-1-472-12735-8

MacCarthy. J. 2014, The Emotional Sphere of Politics, Matador, ISBN 978-1-783-06221-8

Milburn. K. 2019, Generation Left, Polity, ISBN 978-1-509-53224-7

Navarro. J. 2014, Dangerous Personalities, Rodale, ISBN 978-1-635-65336-6

Oborne. P. 2021, The Assault On Truth, Simon & Schuster, ISBN 978-1-398-50100-3

Richards. S. 2017, The Rise Of The Outsiders, Atlantic, ISBN 978-1-786-49142-8

Rickards. J. 2016, The Road To Ruin, Random House, ISBN 978-0-241-18920-7

Spalding. R. 2019, Stealth Wars, Portfolio Penguin, ISBN 978-0-593-08434-2

Stephens. P. 2021, Britain Alone, Faber & Faber, ISBN 978-0-571-34178-8

Strauss et. al. W. 1997, The Fourth Turning, Three Rivers, ISBN 978-0-767-90046-1

Technology.

Jackson. J. 2019, You Are What You Read, Unbound, ISBN 978-1-785-52722-9

Lanier. J. 2018, Ten Arguments For Deleting Your Social Media Account, Random House, ISBN 978-1-529-11240-5

Lewis. A. 2021, The Basics Of Bitcoins And Blockchains, Mango, ISBN 978-1-642-50673-0

Pariser. E. 2011, The Filter Bubble, Penguin, ISBN 978-0-241-95452-2

Suleyman. M. 2023, The Coming Wave, Random House, ISBN 978-1-847-92748-4

Zuboff. S. 2019, The Age Of Surveillance Capitalism, Hachette, ISBN 978-1-781-25685-5

Money

Baker. R. 2005, Capitalism's Achilles Heel, Wiley ISBN978-0-471-64488-9

Goodchild. P. 2007, Theology Of Money, SCM Press, ISBN 978-0-334-04142-9

North. P. 2010, Local Money, Transition, ISBN 978-1-900-32252-2

Rickards. J. 2011, Currency Wars, Portfolio, ISBN 978-1-591-84556-0

Rickards. J. 2015, The Death Of Money, Penguin, ISBN 978-0-670-92370-0

Scott, B, 2013, The Heretic's Guide To Global Finance, Pluto, ISBN978-0-745-33350-2

Change

Brown et al. M. 2021, Paint Your Town Red, Repeater, ISBN 978-1-913-46219-2

Kasumu. S. 2023, The Power Of The Outsider, Hodder & Stoughton, ISBN 978-1-529-39691-1

Prowle (Ed). M. 2023, Reforming UK Public Policy, Routledge, ISBN 978-1-032-06356-0

Senge. P. 1990, The Fifth Discipline, Random House, ISBN 978-0-712-65687-1

Stroud. D. 2021, The Secondary Mod, Kindle Direct, ISBN 978-0-995-65772-4.

Wise. A. 1968, The Day The Queen Flew To Scotland For The Grouse Shooting, Cavalier SBN 340-10770-7

Other stuff

Fukuyama. F. 2019, Identity   Profile, ISBN 978-1-781-25981-8

Mazzucato et. al. M. 2023, The Big Con, Penguin ISBN 978-0-241-57308-2

Rampton et.al. S. 2001, Trust Us We're Experts, Tarcher Putnam, ISBN 978-1-585-42139-1

Rosen. M. 1953, Dignity, Harvard, ISBN 978-0-674-98405-9

Thaler et. al. R. 2008, Nudge, Penguin, ISBN 978-0-141-04001-1

<u>Index</u>

By The Same Author:

2020, Yorkshire, The Case For Independence. ISBN 978-1-80031-899-1

2023, Yorkshire 2027, A Strategy For Tomorrow. ISBN 978-1-80369-765-9

2020, (with D. Clegg & D Philpott), Eight Miles To The Pub. ISBN 978-1-80031-723-9

2019, Beyond Money, A Guide To Sustainable Business. ISBN978-1-78955-828-9

2015, How To Market Yourself In A Week. ISBN 978-0-95763-403-9

2015, (with Vince Golder), The Consummate Professional's Guide To Referral Marketing. ISBN 978-1-78955-339-0

2013, The Story Of Cash Flow, ISBN 978-0-95763-402-2

Blogsite at www.fundamentally.typepad.com

Meet The Author

After graduating as a biologist, then an ecologist, Steve Mullins changed direction to work across a number of corporate boundaries, bringing insight and clarity to many functions and activities.

He started his commercial life as a scientist in R&D, working closely with brand management. An opportunity in marketing gave him the move to become a marketer – cutting his teeth with highly respected brands in the 1970's.

Later he moved to a UK division of a major international confectionery company where he developed new services for integration into the parent company. This included a responsibility for highly specialist market research in sectors which had been poorly reported up to that time.

The job complexity increased when he joined a division of a tobacco giant with the brief to take new ideas and opportunities, sort them, develop them, launch them, manage them to profit and integrate them into the parent company. It was here that his communications skills and genuine understanding of delivering benefits was developed.

Following corporate management, Steve became independent, setting up his own consultancy and partnering with others to deliver business strategy, marketing planning and export support. He also worked with The Business Link, Access to Finance, Train To Gain and a number of government-based support initiatives.

Steve has been officially congratulated on a series of programmes with BBC Radio Berkshire, won the London Brokerage Award for Staff Innovation, the *South & East Building Better Business* run by Barclays Bank, came south-east runner-up in the *Making A Difference* awards hosted by Shell – both latter awards in competition with the major consultancies.

Steve has also delivered CMI Management qualifications to level 5, marked to level 7 and is Certificated to externally assess training centres.

He has been SFEDI accredited, CRB checked, was a Chartered Marketer, a Fellow of the Institute of Management Consultancy, a Fellow of the Royal Society for Arts, a Member of the Institute for Business Ethics, Member of The Richmond Group of Consultants and held directorships with Gerard International Ltd, Business Wealth and Ascot Associates Ltd.

He is now retired.

www.ingramcontent.com/pod-product-compliance
Lightning Source LLC
Chambersburg PA
CBHW031120250726
48655CB00004B/1778